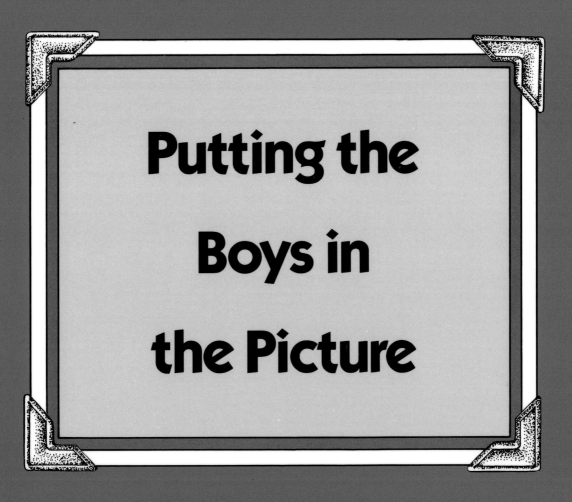

Putting the Boys in the Picture

A Review of Programs
to Promote Sexual Responsibility
Among Young Males

Joy G. Dryfoos

Putting the Boys in the Picture

A Review of Programs to Promote Sexual Responsibility Among Young Males

Joy G. Dryfoos

Network Publications, a division of ETR Associates
Santa Cruz, CA 1988

This book was made possible by a grant from the Carnegie Corporation of New York. The opinions expressed are those of the author and do not necessarily reflect those of the Carnegie Corporation.

10 9 8 7 6 5 4 3 2 1

Cover design: Julia Chiapella

Title No. 370

Library of Congress Cataloging-in-Publication Data

Dryfoos, Joy G.
  Putting the boys in the picture : a review of programs to
promote sexual responsibility among young males / Joy G.Dryfoos.
   p. cm.
   "A report to the Carnegie Corporation, 1988."

  Bibliography: p.
  ISBN 0-941816-55-9
  1. Sex instruction—United States. 2. Sexual ethics for teen-
agers. 3. Teenage boys—United States—Sexual behavior. 4.
Birth control—Study and teaching—United States. I. Carnegie
Corporation of New York. II. Title.
HQ57.D78 1988
306.7'07—dc19   88-15937
            CIP

Contents

Preface

*I*n 1984, Gloria Primm Brown, Program Associate of the Carnegie Corporation, asked me if I would write a "Review of Programs and Services to Foster Responsible Sexual Behavior on the Part of Adolescent Boys." The report was duly submitted and circulated by the foundation to interested parties. Since this effort was started, we have observed a rapidly growing demand for ideas about how to "put the boys in the pregnancy prevention picture."

This book is a revision of the original report. It is being published by Network Publications with support from the Carnegie Corporation. The sustenance of the foundation, and particularly Gloria Primm Brown's commitment to exploring troubling issues surrounding the problem of adolescent pregnancy, are greatly appreciated. The opinions expressed here, however, are those of the author and do not necessarily reflect the opinions of the Carnegie Corporation.

This is the first volume to appear that focuses entirely on pregnancy prevention and young males. However, a small group of practitioners have been promoting male involvement programs for many years, conducting workshops, designing and operating programs and writing articles. This group is centered in the Task Force on Male Involvement in Family Planning and Reproductive Health sponsored by the Population Section of the American Public Health Association.

Many people's names appear in this volume, and that is appropriate when we are talking about programs. Although we can make every effort to extract from our knowledge base certain abstract principles that are translated into recommendations, we always come back to the people doing the work. They are the ones who actually influence the lives of young people, who have the patience and skills to make a difference in their futures. Putting boys into the picture requires caring adults, whether we are talking about condom distribution, family life education, clinics, role modeling, school remediation, employment programs or any of the other interventions described in this book.

I would like to dedicate this book to program people, without whom there would be no programs...and surely no book.

Summary

Sex and Contraception

- Premarital sexual intercourse is a norm for American male adolescents; in some communities, the average age at first coitus is twelve years old.
- The double standard prevails. Boys initiate sex to respond to a physical need while girls do it for romantic reasons.
- The first act of intercourse among males is rarely planned (although it is long anticipated) and more than half use no contraception at the time of initiation.
- About one-fourth of all young sexually active males currently use condoms. However, many boys are too embarrassed to purchase condoms, even in stores where they are openly displayed.
- Adolescent males generally feel they should share the responsibility for pregnancy prevention, but they have difficulty communicating their concerns and do not know how to talk to girls.
- Peers exert heavy influence on young men, especially toward losing virginity.
- Young men express great concern about AIDS but do not appear to be changing behavior.

Existing Programs and Services

- Only half of all high-school-age males have had a sex education course, yet three-fourths of high schools say they offer such courses.
- Males know less about sexuality, contraception and pregnancy than females, even when they have equal access to sex education.
- Over the past decade, repeated efforts have been made to recruit male patients for family planning clinics. The low level of success has been attributed to lack of funding, lack of male staff and negative attitudes on the part of female staff. Many providers believe that males will not seek services in a female-oriented clinic.

- Condom distribution programs are most often cited as effective means for reaching males. One state, Maryland, distributes more than half-a-million condoms a year in 170 sites.
- Outreach and community education directed toward males is being implemented by street workers, peer advocates, teen theater groups, hot lines and media campaigns. Most try to recruit males for clinic programs and/or counseling. Some hand out condoms while others refer males to various community agencies.
- Comprehensive health clinics, including those based in schools, appear to eliminate some of the barriers to utilization by males. These programs provide sexuality counseling, STD screening, contraceptives and general health care, including physical examinations.

Support and Evaluation

- Many national organizations have launched male involvement initiatives using the media, mentoring, youth agencies, schools and churches. Some are in the process of developing new strategies.
- In 1984, the Office of Family Planning (Title X, DHHS) awarded small, supplemental, one-time grants through regional offices to twenty agencies for the initiation of male involvement programs. Few of these programs survived after the funding stopped.
- Current Office of Family Planning policies act as a deterrent to serving males. Clinics may *not* count males as patients. The American Public Health Association recently adopted a policy opposing this practice.
- Financial support for male programs is minimal. Except for the Title X grants, few sources of government funds are available for free-standing programs. Comprehensive health clinics can use Medicaid funds for eligible young males. State health funds can be used for health services in schools and clinics.
- Evaluation of the impact of male involvement programs is almost nonexistent. Given the difficulty of measuring male fertility rates, this is not surprising. A few programs have counts of users or contacts. Condom distribution programs conducted in the 1960's claimed reductions in fertility rates in rural counties. Several school-related clinics have demonstrated improvement in contraceptive use among young male students.

Need for Services

- Of the 15.6 million young men in the U.S. aged 14 to 21, at least 10 million have had sexual intercourse.
- The total number of teenage fathers is unknown. In 1984, only 89,000 were reported

(the age was not reported for 37% of fathers of babies of teen mothers).

- Knowledge of the characteristics of teen fathers is limited. Unless self-identified, fathers remain "shadow figures." Those who have been studied appear to be similar to teen mothers: they are disadvantaged, experience failure in school and lack employment skills. Most are about two years older than their partners. Most claim they did not want the pregnancy to occur.
- The rationale for increasing efforts to involve males in pregnancy prevention includes the following points: although boys feel a great deal of pressure to initiate sex at an early age, they are not mature enough to deal with emotional relationships, do not have access to contraception and lack cognitive ability to plan for the future. To share responsibility for pregnancy prevention, boys need communication skills.
- Lack of motivation to prevent pregnancy among disadvantaged young males may be attributed to the absence of life options.
- Adolescents at highest risk of becoming teenage fathers have the least potential for providing for a family. Improvement in employment opportunities is critical both for motivating young men to avoid early parenthood and for ameliorating the quality of life for those who do become fathers.
- Some adolescents "make it" despite all odds. Research shows that a caring adult— a parent, teacher or another person—had a strong influence on their success.

*R*ecommendations

- For disadvantaged young men at high risk of paternity, there must be an improvement in the prospects for a better life before pregnancy prevention messages will have any effect. This means major long-term institutional changes must take place so young men can complete high school, learn skills and obtain jobs.
- For all boys, there are several short-term strategies that may enhance their capacities to become more sexually responsible and enjoy more mature relationships with peers, partners and parents:
  1. Large-scale free confidential condom distribution.
  2. Effective male service components provided by family planning clinics, and clinic personnel trained to implement male programs.
  3. Expansion of comprehensive school and community multi-service programs to include family planning for boys and girls.
  4. Promotion of the boys' role in decision making and communication through social-skills training, media campaigns, role models, recreational services and general consciousness raising.
- While common sense criteria indicate many promising approaches to reaching males, research that compares the effectiveness of alternative program components is essential. Many recent community-wide and/or comprehensive service efforts should have an impact on young men as well as young women.

ix

- Analysis of national survey data could shed some additional light on the determinants of early paternity, sexual activity and contraceptive use among males.
- Program development in the United States could be enhanced by sharing information on program models with program administrators from other countries where services for males are more heavily utilized.
- No single program will solve the problem of adolescent pregnancy. A whole package of programs calling for commitment at the community, state and national levels to a healthy future for youth is required.

I
Introduction

*O*ver the past decade, the outpouring of reports, articles, conferences, rhetoric and legislation concerning adolescent pregnancy has been impressive. However, until quite recently, almost all the attention has been focused on females. This is not surprising since girls suffer the direct consequences of unprotected intercourse. But as pregnancy rates remain intractable despite efforts to help girls "say no" or use contraception, and as the importance of early prevention interventions becomes more salient, there is a growing consciousness that unless boys are put into the picture, the problem cannot be solved. The threat of AIDS has added an unprecedented urgency to the messages of prevention.

Awareness is a good first step in the male involvement process. If we knew of effective interventions, the second step would logically be program development. The Panel on Adolescent Pregnancy and Childbearing appointed by the National Academy of Sciences recently reported on its two-year, in-depth study of the issues. The development and evaluation of condom distribution programs was the only male-specific intervention mentioned. The absence of more information about males in the report is attributed to

> ...the lack of research on males...reflecting the fact that policy makers, service providers, parents, and teenagers themselves have traditionally regarded adolescent pregnancy and childbearing as a female problem (Hayes, 1987).

If we knew how to convince all young men to take responsibility for their sexual behavior, it is likely that adolescent pregnancy rates would decrease, as would the threat of AIDS. It has been documented that young women with a strong commitment to future careers and assurance that they can carry out their life goals are not often teenage mothers. Perhaps the same attributes can be applied to young men. Perhaps teenage males who are succeeding in school and have a real sense of the future are more careful about their sexual behavior than those whose lives hold little hope of opportunity.

An underlying assumption of this book is that adolescent pregnancy is a symptom of larger societal problems. The issues of sexuality and reproduction cannot be disassociated from the issues of disadvantage, racism and inequity. The behavior under investigation is taking place in a rapidly deteriorating social environment, with growing threats of homelessness, alienation, racial strife, violence, drugs and AIDS. Do these phenomena "cause" pregnancy or are they a consequence of early childbearing?

One reason the causation theories for male sexual behavior are difficult to prove is that the essential outcome, paternity, is not easily established. Some boys do not know that they have become fathers. Others deny it. As we shall see, many more teenage females than males report pregnancies. Although we know that most teen fathers are two years older than teen mothers, the known pregnancy rates for males are clearly an undercount.

Despite the evaluation gap, it is possible to identify some efforts that meet the test of common sense: if more young boys are reached by these interventions, it is likely that they will become more responsible about their sexual behavior and concerned about the consequences of their acts. That is the test that will be applied in this book. The evaluation gap is applicable not only to the subject of male involvement in prevention of adolescent pregnancy; it is pervasive in social science literature, even for subjects with measurable outcomes such as school retention and employability.

This book begins with a brief review of current literature on male involvement from which many of the findings and program ideas reported here were compiled. A short essay on the self-reported life experiences of adolescent males is followed with statistical data on the social and economic status of U.S. adolescents. The research on the determinants of adolescent pregnancy—e.g., initiation of sexual activity, use of contraception and attitudes toward pregnancy, and the experience of fatherhood—is reviewed from the point of view of understanding adolescent male roles.

Programs directed toward males are discussed next. Strategies of organizations promoting male involvement and their sources of financial support are summarized. The final section presents preliminary recommendations directed toward enhancing the capacity and motivation for boys to become more sexually responsible. Priorities for action are included. The preceding summary outlines the salient points from each section.

A major shortcoming of the data presented in this book is that they only come in two colors: Black and White. We do not have access to much information about socio-economic and cultural differences. This fact should be kept in mind when reviewing the statistical findings and readers should be careful not to generalize about racial groups.

Literature
Review

*A*lthough there are an increasing number of books about adolescent sexuality and pregnancy in the United States, no one book focuses on adolescent males. Either the subject of the volume is males in general (Swanson and Forrest, 1984), adolescent fathers (Lamb and Elster, 1985) or adolescent pregnancy with emphasis on females (Chilman, 1983; Smith, 1985; Stuart, 1982). Recent articles about programs and services directed toward young males are scarce. A computer search revealed 400 entries, mostly outdated, on the subject of males and family planning. Many were about psychology or sterilization. Several described programs in developing countries. A *Review and Annotated Bibliography of Literature on Male Involvement in Family Planning* was produced by the National Institute for Community Development (NICD) under contract with the Office of Family Planning in January of 1978. The review was broad; few studies dealt with adolescents and most were conducted over a decade ago. However, some of the articles cited in this report were identified from that source.

The published literature reviewed by NICD described eighteen programs which offered family planning services for men, categorized in four areas: reproductive health, education and counseling, vasectomy services and condom distribution. NICD concludes:

> Because not every male program has met with unqualified success, there are some unanswered questions about the specific factors...necessary for successful male family planning programs. The published literature gives no indication that 'successful' programs are being studied in any systematic or comprehensive way. It may be that evaluation studies have been or are being conducted, because it is clear from...conversations and site visits that much more is going on than is reflected in the published literature and government reports.

This perceptive comment predicts the current situation. Ten years later, virtually no program evaluations have emerged despite new activity regarding male involvement in the field.

The more recently published Swanson-Forrest volume *Men's Reproductive Health*

Care is a collection of papers developed from a task force on male involvement of the American Public Health Association. The book provides information and guidelines for health professionals on men's reproductive health concerns, including anatomy, physiology, sexuality, sex roles and fertility control. There are contributions from the fields of urology, nursing, occupational health, family planning, and sexuality counseling. This material is useful for practitioners, but has little program analysis and almost no mention of teenagers. In her chapter "Shared Contraception" Swanson promotes the concept of joint participation in activities related to acquisition, use, and consequences of contraception. She reminds primary care clinicians to encourage treatment of couples, to discuss their joint concerns and to enlighten them about myths of contraception. She suggests that clinicians share the cultural assumptions of their patients (e.g., Blacks should be treated by Blacks), and present contraceptive methods in a way that does not threaten "machismo" among Hispanic males. Physicians should be aware of life cycle events and introduce the subject of contraception to patients at developmentally appropriate times.

Rappaport's chapter "Family Planning: Helping Men Ask for Help" proposes techniques to counter the problem that almost no programs exist for men who want assistance. From his own experience, he warns clinics to adopt neither the female model nor the "macho" model but to develop a new strategy of innovative counseling that confronts the barriers erected by traditional male role socialization. He believes men need help in expressing their emotions.

Scales and Beckstein, in a volume edited by Stuart (1982), do consider adolescents: "From Macho to Mutuality: Helping Young Men Make Effective Decisions about Sex, Contraception and Pregnancy." This chapter contains the most comprehensive statement about the effectiveness of various interventions and includes material incorporated in sections that follow. The authors review research on men's sexual decision making in the context of moral development and then summarize studies on initiation of intercourse, communication between partners, use of and attitudes about contraceptives, and male participation in pregnancy resolution. They conclude that young men need to be offered "opportunities for reasoning about sexual issues in nonthreatening situations to counteract the tendency for men to reason at less morally mature levels than women when considering sex." They support development of programs with well trained adult male staff, father and son workshops, and more comprehensive programs with employment and health services. "Most important, our efforts must be based on talking about men's *rights* as well as...their responsibilities...we point the finger of blame at the 'irresponsible,' 'uncaring,' 'selfish' man...'incapable' of the prevention of unplanned pregnancy." They propose more ego-enhancing approaches and less negative stereotyping by stressing the *right* to use a condom, to be protected against STDs, to express physical and verbal affection to other men, to friendship without sex, to masturbation. The chapter concludes with 48 references; none include program reviews.

The Smith (1985) volume on adolescent reproductive health includes the chapter "Adolescent Male Reproduction: A Point of Focus" written by Smith and Kolenda. Their assumption is that the role of adolescent males in reproductive health and sexuality has not been adequately addressed (an assumption well documented in this literature review). After a brief summary of studies on adolescent male sexual behavior and attitudes toward contraception, the authors present a useful discussion of male services. They start by reminding us that "while the adolescent...male has a strong sensual orientation, that does not immediately suggest that he has a concomitant or parallel interest in sexual health." Thus, the demand by high risk boys for sexual health programs is minimal.

Smith (1985) proposes several approaches that might increase male participation in family planning. These include: combining sexual health with a broad range of general health services, offering referrals for other problems, altering clinic environments, conducting staff training to heighten sensitivity to male needs, aggressively marketing condoms and improving partner communication. Although these approaches have not been evaluated, they are based on behavioral research findings, observations, and common sense. Many of her suggestions are incorporated into the recommendations section of this report. The chapter concludes with ideas about counseling males on sexual responsibility.

Chilman (1983), in her exhaustive treatment of adolescent sexuality (perhaps the most comprehensive overview), asserts at the outset the importance of including males in the discussion of these issues:

> Although males and females have their special vulnerabilities and strengths and although sexuality has somewhat different meanings for each sex, research about adolescent sexuality and resultant policies and programs rarely considers both sexes and rarely takes into account their likenesses as well as their differences. An overemphasis is placed on female needs and characteristics. An unfortunate aspect of this tendency is to underrate the importance and responsibility of males in sexual partnerships and to underplay the importance of interpersonal partnerships between the sexes. This lack of sufficient attention to males can create difficulties for any age group; it is particularly apt to do so for impressionable adolescents.

Chilman next explains how adolescent sexuality is shaped through social-psychological characteristics of the family, socio-cultural forces, values and norms, communities and institutions. She believes the effects of our current economic conditions and employment opportunities on male and female identity, goals, values and behaviors are profound. Pointing out the massive changes that have taken place between 1960 and 1980, she feels society offers less clear directions to young people today.

Unfortunately, Chilman does not devote a chapter exclusively to adolescent males, leaving the reader to sift through her research overviews to find relevant sentences. In an interesting chapter on the biology of adolescents, she states:

> The male's need to prove himself sexually is enhanced by a culture that, despite the feminist equal rights movement, still tends to equate adequate masculinity with many forms of achievement on the part of the male...The fact remains that coitus centrally involves aggressive male penetration and female receptivity.

7

As Chilman describes the situation, males readily experience sexual arousal during the everyday course of their lives and view sexuality in a "pleasure-orienting, assertive, achieving, unitary and less personal fashion" than girls do.

Chilman presents an overview of psychological literature on sexual development and a discussion of trends in sexual attitudes and practices. In a chapter on adolescent parents, she concludes that many communities fall short of providing quality counseling and advocacy that young male parents need. Gilchrist and Schinke, in their chapter on counseling adolescents about sexuality apply techniques of life-skills enhancement to teach young boys and girls decision making and problem solving, creating greater sexual responsibility. In a section on contraceptive services, Chilman mentions the poor treatment accorded males in most birth control clinics and suggests clinics include male partners in rap sessions and in their female partner's physical examination and give them physicals (particularly for VD screening) and instructions in the technique of withdrawal and condom use. She recommends distribution of condoms, foams and jellies in public restrooms and gas stations and in schools and recreation centers where young people congregate. She proposes hiring males to conduct research for clinics and including boys in parent communication workshops. She, too, refers to staff sensitivity to males and the need for in-service training. Giving males a sense of responsibility and making them a copartner in birth control should be a high priority.

The Chilman book ends with a thoughtful chapter on implications for public policies. Once again she cites the social environmental deficits resulting in escalating rates of out-of-wedlock childbearing among disadvantaged youth. She calls for improved employment opportunities, educational enhancement and reform of welfare policies that create barriers to maintaining two-parent families and involving young fathers. The book stresses the importance of working with the whole person in the context of a total life situation.

Many common themes run through the literature on male involvement, confirming ideas presented in interviews and site visits. The subject of adolescent males is not accorded the same importance as the subject of adolescent females; less is known about services for males (perhaps because less is being done to help males). There appears to be a consensus about what needs to be done: helping young men get in touch with their feelings; involving them in some form of medical health care to initiate sexuality counseling and referral; giving them access to contraceptive methods; altering delivery mechanisms to make them more appropriate; and generally assisting young males to understand that they are partners in the sexual act and pregnancy prevention. The literature stresses the importance of culturally relevant outreach to male adolescents but presents little evidence to back up the innovative counseling ideas.

What
Adolescent
Males
Say

What do boys have to say about the issue of male involvement? Discussions with small groups of young males, review of several ethnographic studies, and interviews with knowledgeable informants have revealed some strong messages. In response to the question, "What do young men need in order to convince them to 'behave' responsibly?" the consensus is "jobs." To put the situation in the bleakest light, one Black social worker told me,

> I'd have to be crazy to go up to Harlem and tell those guys who are standing around on street corners to stop doing it. They have nothing else going for them; most of them have never had a job and the way things are going, they never will.

This is, of course, the worst case. Exploring it a little further, we can look at the life history of a group of teen fathers (Sullivan, 1985). Growing up in intense poverty, surrounded by relatives (particularly sisters) who were teen parents and often dependent on welfare, few had ever had any relationship with their fathers. Early sex "results from the large amount of time that is neither structured nor supervised by adults"—taking place in empty apartments during school hours. There is no imperative to attend school. Escape from boredom and/or group pressure toward delinquency are alleviated through being with girls. Petty street crime is a way of life and those who follow that course usually have periods of incarceration. The preferred path is low level drug dealing—if carefully conducted, jail is avoided and a full-time career may ensue.

A recent report from the Teen Father Collaborative, a group of eight father involvement programs, characterized the participants as:

> A group confronted by a multitude of problems—poverty, unemployment and lack of skills and education—suffering from low self-esteem as a result of their inability to find work and their dismal outlook for the future (Sanders and Rosen, 1987).

9

These themes are reiterated in the works of contemporary ethnologists. Describing the daily life of the Hallway Hangers, a gang of mostly White male teenagers who hang out around a public housing project, MacLeod (1987) points to an existence marked by:

> ...unrelieved boredom and monotony...these boys are generally out of work, out of school and out of money. In search of employment or a fast buck on the street, high or drunk a good deal of the time, many are preoccupied with staying out of prison, a struggle some have already lost, and with surviving from one day to the next.

Interviews with more upwardly mobile achievement-oriented young men from Detroit documented the impact of drug traffic. "You can't leave school without being confronted by drug peddlers. They are everywhere. The guys who do it (as well as some girls) always have a lot of cash." Crime accompanies the drug trade and the amount of knifing and shooting going on in Detroit makes the trip to and from school fraught with danger. Guards have been hired to frisk all students as they enter school.

These boys, who were apparently good students, had no intention of becoming teen fathers. They aspired to a variety of professions and many referred to adults, particularly teachers, who were helping them. Yet most of them expressed grave doubts about their prospects. They cited the 71 percent teen unemployment rate in Detroit and several recounted frustrating experiences with job seeking.

Does aspiration make the difference between those who become fathers and those who don't? One young man in another setting told me proudly, "If I ever got a girl pregnant, my mother would *kill* me!" This young man placed high value on school achievement and was already trying to decide to which Ivy League college he should apply. He considered girls who were promiscuous far beneath him, referring to them as "sluts."

Class structure clearly enters into these distinctions. However, the teen fathers who come from truly deprived backgrounds *also* claimed they too did not intend to become fathers (Sullivan, 1985). Yet despite taking sex education courses in school, none practiced birth control, even after fatherhood. Condoms (which they called "bags") received very low ratings; a few tried to practice withdrawal but it wasn't pleasurable. The older girls they had sex with used pills. Unfortunately, when they had sex with younger girls, no one used any protection and thus the pregnancy.

Despite their marginal and uncertain relationships to the girl whom they impregnated, abortion was not considered an option. Their opposition to abortion appeared to be based on the following analysis: *they* might never have been born if *their* parents planned parenthood on the basis of economic preparedness. As Sullivan describes it, the desire to escape poverty coexists with the desire to affirm life in the face of poverty.

Repeatedly, boys who were interviewed mentioned ignorance as a particularly important barrier for younger teens of both sexes (Darabi, 1985). "People don't know how to get protection or how to use it." "Sex is never planned or expected...it just happens." However, boys seemed more likely than girls to report that their parents promoted contraception; one mother told her son, "I heard you have a girl, be careful!" A father warned, "It's your business, but remember the consequences, it will be your problem."

The pressure on boys to lose their virginity is felt from casual and close friends, older brothers and even fathers. "You're a chump if you don't do it." "All younger guys want is sex, sex, sex. They make girls think they'll stay with them, but once it's over, they go to their best friend." "Sex is like drinking water—if I can have it, I'll take it and boom then comes the baby."

In summary, the life experience of adolescent males mirrors that of adolescent females; for young people who are achieving in school and feel their future prospects are good, early paternity is not an issue. For those who are failing in school, who are ignorant about reproduction, who operate outside the norms of society, pregnancy does not become an issue until confrontation with the reality of the subsequent birth. While the pregnancies are unplanned, many of these disadvantaged young men assume responsibility for the child and try to muster whatever financial and emotional support they can scrape together. Like teenage mothers, teenage fathers appear to be very proud of their offspring, one accomplishment in a sea of frustrations.

Many, if not most, young men fall somewhere between the two extremes—the achievers who almost never become young fathers and the failures, many of whom have children while adolescents. Yet given the norms of early sexual initiation, almost all boys are at risk of STDs and given the absence of contraception, many are at risk of early paternity.

Developmental Issues

*W*hether the sex drive attributed to young boys is biologically or culturally determined has not been resolved (Smith, 1985; Chilman, 1983; Gordon, 1979). There is ample evidence that boys have nocturnal emissions and begin to masturbate at early ages. In one view, "when adolescent boys learn that their culture views masturbation as childish...they are pressured into precocious sexual behavior" (Calderwood, 1984). Throughout childhood, boys are pushed to conform with the gender role of aggressiveness, athletic performance, dominance and competitiveness. They are programmed to perform and are measured by their performance unlike girls who are more likely to be measured by their attractiveness and personality.

Recent research on the effect of hormones on adolescent sexuality has shed new insights into male-female differences. Udry and colleagues (1985) studied a small sample of White 8th to 10th graders in one community to determine any relationship between hormonal levels and their sexual development and experience. The research suggests that hormones (testosterone) have a direct and intense effect on young males, stimulating sexual behavior. For females, the effect is indirect and spread over many years. Hormones stimulate pubertal development, which in turn effects sexual behavior. Thus, if a girl develops pubic hair and breasts, she begins to date, but motivation for actual coitus is dependent on social rather than biological processes. Motivation for coitus among boys, Udry believes, stems from hormone levels, which provide a "more powerful jolt."

Thus the double standard is inherent in both the social environment and the biological imperatives in which American adolescents grow up: boys are expected to express their sexual identity by acting it out, "doing it," while girls are urged to suppress their sexuality. Parents encourage this duality by accepting premarital behavior among boys and condemning it among girls. While the new sexual scene has somewhat lessened this differential treatment, many otherwise liberated families still portray the same messages to their youngsters that their parents portrayed to them. Boys may have an even harder time establishing their sexual roles today in the absence of positive male role models; the only adult males they meet at home are their mother's boyfriends who may be quite temporary in the family scene. At the same time, their own fathers may be openly acting out with a series of women who are not candidates for marriage.

Adolescent boys are under great pressure, trying to establish their sexual and psychological identities in stressful family, social and school situations. The morbidity and mortality rates give evidence to the resulting problems: boys are seen in guidance clinics three times as often as girls; they outnumber girls in mental institutions by 150 percent (Calderwood, 1984). Suicide rates are five times higher for young males (20.2 per 100,000) than for young females (4.3), and as would be expected, accident and mortality rates are much higher as well (Statistical Abstract, 1984).

Young boys are socialized to "score" as soon as they can, with little consideration for the object of the event or the feelings of the partner who "will probably provide only a physical release rather than an emotional attachment" (Smith, 1985). In many peer groups, losing one's virginity is the required rite of passage for group acceptance. This peer group pressure runs a counter-point to rebellion against authority, so that both being accepted by friends and doing something parents wouldn't approve of (overtly) can be accomplished in one swift act of intercourse. Only very strong religious beliefs can deter this experience, once the opportunity presents itself. Among some cultural groups, even religiosity is not a deterrent.

In order to relate the immediate gratification to the long- term consequence, a young boy must reach a level of cognitive development whereby he is capable of abstract thought. We know some young people grow up physically yet lack the skills and moral development necessary for assuming adult roles. We also should recognize that most young people *do* act responsibly even though there has been no national commitment to helping them deal with sexuality issues.

How then do we teach all young men to be sexually responsible? It appears we must start by recognizing the strong drive for initiating sexual intercourse. It does not matter whether this drive is biological or sociological, the important point is that boys feel it and want to do something about it. The first level of response should probably be to understand what is going on and help youngsters discover their own bodies, how they function and what their real needs are. Secondly, males must be taught as much about sexuality, contraception and pregnancy as girls are. They need to be given shared responsibility for the relationship and taught how to care for and respect their partners (as well as their same sex friends).

Any interventions initiated must be developmentally appropriate.

Where the Boys Are

*O*ur nation includes 15.6 million young men, aged 14 to 21, who may be considered as potential partners of the 15.1 million females of the same age (U.S. Bureau of the Census, 1986a). The number of younger adolescent boys is decreasing: the size of the cohort of 14 to 17 year olds dropped by 13 percent since 1975 while the 18 to 21 year old cohort decreased by five percent. The sex ratio differs by race: White males outnumber White females in all age groups to age 35 while for Blacks, the ratio is equal for 15 to 19 year olds but decreases to 93 males per 100 females for 20-24 year old Blacks and 89 males per 100 females for 25-29 year-old Blacks. This differential sex ratio limits the marriage market for young Black women.

According to the 1985 census, 70 percent of young U.S. males (aged 14-21) are currently enrolled in school: 7.6 million are still in high school and 2.8 million are in college. Of the remainder, 3.0 million have completed high school and 1.4 million are not enrolled and have not completed high school (U.S. Bureau of the Census, 1986b). (School enrollment data are available for 14.8 million males in 1985, leaving the rest unaccounted for.) The dropout rate based on Census data is about 10 percent.

Other surveys show higher dropout rates than the Census. According to data from the High School and Beyond study, about 15 percent of all males dropped out of high school between their sophomore and senior years. Minority youngsters were more likely to drop out (or be dropped out). Some 20 percent of Black and 18 percent of Hispanic young males did not graduate, compared to 13 percent of Whites and 4 percent of Asian-Americans in this group (Barro and Kolstad, 1987). For males, dropping out is associated with low socio-economic status, living in an urban community, not being in an academic high school and having low grades in school. However, the most significant variables are being married and/or having children, for males as well as for females:

Marital and parenting status of males:	Probability of males dropping out:
Married, with children	74.8%
Unmarried, with children	45.3%
Married, no children	59.3%
Unmarried, no children	11.2%

Barro and Kolstad found the probability of dropping out among males was twice as high if they were married, and four times as high if they had children, even when all other personal, family and school variables were held constant. The effect was greatest for White and Hispanic males. The authors are careful to point out that we do not know the timing of these events (marriage, children, dropping out), but these data show the experiences are highly related. Marsiglio (1987) suggests some of those who dropped out of school and became fathers were already disconnected from the educational system and did not perceive of fatherhood as a barrier to future opportunity (which was already limited).

Of the 4.1 million young men aged 16 to 19 in the labor force, 800,000 (19.5%) were unemployed in 1985 (U.S. Bureau of the Census, 1986a). Unemployment rates were highest among young and minority males:

Age	White	Black
Age 16-19	16.6%	41.0%
Age 20-24	9.7%	23.6%

It is difficult to sort out the overlap between unemployment, school dropout and labor force participation. Table 1 presents the most recent data from the Current Population Survey. It shows the major activity of young people according to their sex and race during one week of a survey. More than half of 16 to 21 year olds were attending school, many still in high school. About three out of five young White males were in the labor force, a higher rate than for Black males (47%). Some 18 percent of White males were both in school and employed, compared to only six percent of Blacks. Unemployment rates defined for this table were relatively low; 10 percent of White males and 18 percent of Black males were both in the labor force and unemployed. However, a high proportion of Blacks were not in the labor force (54%) and many of those young men were also not in school. Almost one in ten Black males were neither in the labor force nor in school compared to one in twenty White males.

At the bottom of the table are figures just for dropouts. Of the 1.3 million White male dropouts, almost two-thirds were employed, 20 percent were unemployed and 16 percent were not in the labor force. For the quarter of a million Black male dropouts, only 29 percent were employed, 33 percent were unemployed and 38 percent were not in the labor force. The patterns for females were similar, with young Black women showing the highest unemployment and lowest labor force participation rates.

More than two million young males, one in six of those aged 15-21, reside in poverty level households, including 12 percent of White males, 38 percent of Black males and 28 percent of Spanish origin males (U.S. Bureau of the Census, 1987). However, for those who are unemployed, poverty rates are double. These disadvantaged people are at an increased

15

Table 1				
Percent Distribution by Major Activity During Survey Week for Persons Aged 16 to 21, by Sex and Race, 1983 (Numbers in 000s)				
	Males		**Females**	
	White	Black	White	Black
Total	9,023	1,556	8,088	1,547
Percent of total	100%	100%	100%	100%
Major activity				
Going to school	**56**	**56**	**59**	**60**
High school	37	44	36	40
Other school	19	12	23	20
In labor force	**60**	**47**	**56**	**34**
Employed	50	29	49	21
In school	18	6	20	6
Not in school	32	23	30	15
Graduated	23	18	24	13
Dropout	9	5	6	2
Unemployed	10	18	7	13
In school	4	6	3	4
Not in school	6	12	4	9
Graduated	3	7	2	6
Dropout	3	5	2	3
Not in labor force	**39**	**54**	**42**	**66**
In school	34	45	35	50
Not in school	5	9	7	16
Graduated	3	3	3	8
Dropout	2	6	4	8
Dropouts	1,324	246	908	199
Percent of total	100%	100%	100%	100%
Employed	64	29	53	14
Unemployed	20	33	17	24
Not in labor force	16	38	30	62

Source: U.S. Bureau of the Census, Current Population Reports, Series P-60, No. 147, *Characteristics of the Population Below the Poverty Level: 1983*, USGPO, Washington, D.C. 1985, extrapolated form data in Table 28, p.113. Percents may not add to 100 since totals in columns did not add.

risk of high school dropout, lack of employment and based on what is known about early childbearing, high incidence of unplanned out-of-wedlock fatherhood.

Recent work by Berlin and Sum (1988) has documented the interrelationships between high dropout and unemployment rates and low basic skills. Among 12-15 year old students who were in the lowest quintile (20%) of basic skills, one-fifth dropped out within two years compared to only three percent with the highest scores. Male income status reflects both differences in basic academic skills levels and high school graduation. Among 20-23 year old dropouts with low academic skills, their average income was 43 percent of the income of high school graduates with high academic skills. Low skills graduates achieved 56 percent of the highest income and high skills dropouts, 85 percent. Thus academic skills are an even more significant predictor of earnings than high school graduation.

II
Sexual Activity Among Young Males

*M*ore than three-fourths of all young males reported in a 1984 National Longitudinal Survey of Youth (NLSY) that they had experienced sexual intercourse while in their teenage years (Marsiglio and Mott, 1986). This is an even higher figure than presented by the Johns Hopkins Survey of U.S. Teenagers in 1979, when two-thirds of metropolitan unmarried males aged 17 to 21 said that they were no longer virgins (Zelnik and Kantner, 1980). Table 2 presents data from the NLSY, showing the cumulative percent of males and females by race/ethnicity, according to the ages at which they said they had first coitus. Among White males, the proportion having had intercourse increases gradually with age from 13 percent of 14 year olds (by age 15) to 76 percent of 18 year olds. The proportions for Hispanic males are similar, ranging from 19 to 72 percent. At each age, the rates are substantially higher for Black males, ranging from 45 percent to 96 percent. The rates for females are lower for every group and age by 10 to 20 percent.

Table 2
Cumulative Percent Sexually Active by Age 15-19
by Race/Ethnicity

Age of 1st Coitus	Males			Females		
	White %	Black %	Hispanic %	White %	Black %	Hispanic %
15*	13	45	19	6	10	6
16	24	65	33	13	23	14
17	44	82	52	28	45	26
18	61	91	60	45	62	40
19	76	96	72	64	80	55
* by age 15						

Source: Marsiglio and Mott, 1986, Table 5.

21

Clearly Black youngsters initiate sexual intercourse earlier than White and Hispanic youngsters. However, an examination of the data suggests premarital sexual intercourse by age 18 is normative behavior for the majority of U.S. boys. The mean age for first intercourse for all males is 16.3, more than a year younger than the mean age for females, which is 17.4. The determinants of early sexual intercourse are similar for boys and girls: low maternal education, low educational expectations, use of drugs and alcohol, low basic skills and infrequent church attendance (Mott, 1983).

In the earlier Johns Hopkins Survey, sexually active females said their first sexual partners were older than they by close to three years. Yet the males in that survey said they had their first sexual experience with girls who were nearly one year older than they. These data and interview findings suggest that older experienced girls may initiate younger boys who, as they age, initiate younger girls. Thus, a small number of older girls may be responsible for initiating a large number of young boys.

Boys are more likely to describe their first partner as a friend or pick-up, while girls perceive this first partner as a fiancé or steady date. The differences are striking. In the Johns Hopkins Survey, close to 90 percent of teenaged females characterized their first relationship as "engaged, going steady or dating" compared to 37 percent of males (Zelnik and Shah, 1983). Only 10 percent of females reported the first sexual relationship was with a friend or someone recently met compared to 63 percent of the males. Recent data from smaller surveys indicate that first intercourse is often unwanted, not only for girls who have been abused and raped, but for boys who reported that they did not actually want to get involved in sex at the time of the experience (Moore, 1986).

For boys, the seriousness of the relationship with a partner increases with age. For most who initiate sex at 14 or younger, first intercourse is a casual affair. This does not mean boys do not plan their first sexual encounters. Indeed, literature and films are replete with anecdotes about the anticipation of sexual debut, particularly for males. Males were more likely to describe their first intercourse as planned than females, especially when the relationship was described as between friends or with someone recently met.

The Johns-Hopkins study shows that most young males have experienced sexual intercourse by the time they are out of high school, and many have initiated sex while still in junior high school. The double standard prevails; young males enter their sexual lives purposively, at early ages, seeking a casual partner who will make it possible for them to lose their virginity and enter manhood (at least symbolically). Girls appear to cling to the romantic tradition of being seduced or being so madly in love that they allow themselves to "go all the way." These differences have important implications for interventions. For example, "saying no" programs may have two messages: telling girls "say no to boys" and boys to "say no to yourself."

Early initiation of sexual intercourse is shown in other studies of selected populations. A non-random sample of Black male teenagers in Baltimore schools yielded rates of sexual experiences of 81 percent for those aged 14 and under and 92 percent for 15 to 19 year olds, with a mean age of first coitus under 12 years old (Clark *et al.*, 1984). This pattern of very early sexual debut among minority youngsters in poverty areas confirms earlier studies from the mid-1970's (Finkel, 1975). For those of us who grew up in Middle American suburban communities, it is mind-boggling to think about an environment in which virtually all boys are expected to have sex *before* they are in high school. But this may not be a new phenomenon; Kinsey could not find in low-income White communities "a solitary male who had not had sexual relations by the time he was 16 or 17" in his 1948 sample!

Attitudes Toward Sexual Initiation

*T*he Baltimore study asked respondents what age they thought was best for having sex the first time (Zabin, 1984). Interestingly, most boys mentioned an age that was older than when they had first initiated intercourse. The younger they were at the time of the survey, the more likely they were to think they had started too early. Those (few) who were still virgins, selected a "best age" three years older than those who were not.

The authors surmise from these findings that attitudes toward the timing of sex are not sufficiently strong to influence behavior, suggesting that opportunities at the moment may be more important determinants than beliefs. Among those boys who had already experienced intercourse, fully one-fourth thought premarital sex was wrong. As would be expected, virgins were more disapproving of sex prior to marriage than non-virgins.

A study of young Hispanics in New York City revealed strong pressures from fathers and other male relatives to initiate sex at early ages, verifying the "macho" ideology believed to dominate in some Hispanic cultural groups (Darabi, 1984). This situation was described by one boy as follows: "I was at a party with my older brother and he told me to have sex so people wouldn't think I was a faggot." In these same families, girls are closely monitored to make sure they preserve their virginity, thus maintaining a strong double standard that appears to produce ambivalence, guilt and covert sexual relationships. Many Hispanic girls appear at neighborhood family planning clinics for initial visits for pregnancy tests; they express great fears about confidentiality and parental notification.

Estimate of Number of Sexually Active Young Males

About 6.1 million boys ages 15 to 19 are estimated to be sexually active, based on survey data applied to recent population figures. In addition, as shown on Table 3, there are at least half a million boys ages 14 and under who have had sexual relations and more than 3.3 million 20 and 21 year old men who could be partners for sexually active girls. Since premarital intercourse appears to be a norm for U.S. males, the target population for interventions encompasses all 22 million males aged 10 to 21, including 8.8 million 10 to 14 year olds, who are at prime risk of initiating sex in the near future. Of these young men, at least 10 million are currently sexually active.

Table 3
Estimated Number of Males, Age 10 to 21
Sexually Active, 1985

Age group	Population (000s)	Percent Sexually Active (%)	Estimated Number Sexually Active (000s)
10-14	8,762	6	526
15-19	9,445	64	6,139
20-21	4,050	83	3,362
Total	22,257	45	10,027

Source: Population: U.S. Bureau of Census, 1986a. Percent sexually active: extrapolated from Marsiglio and Mott, 1986

The concept of "need" does not appear to have the same intuitive meaning when applied to boys as it does for girls. We assume sexually active girls "need" specific services, particularly contraceptive services and counseling, to help them control their fertility. An entire delivery system has been built around this concept and annual counts determine how well the system is being used. Tracking males in "need" of family planning and their

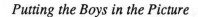

utilization of contraception is much more difficult. It is unlikely (but not impossible) that a strategy will be promulgated enabling every boy to enter into a system of medical care to fill his need for fertility control services.

III
Contraception

While most young males (aged 17-21) reported they did not plan their first sexual encounter, 44 percent had used a contraceptive method and 22 percent had a partner who used a prescription method the first time (Zelnik, 1983). The older the boy was at first intercourse, the more often he reported using a method. As would be expected, a very high proportion of male users used male methods, condoms or withdrawal. Surprisingly, planning status had little effect on type of method used among males but females who had planned their first intercourse were more likely to use pills than non-planners.

Still, among those who planned the first intercourse, 48 percent of White males and 54 percent of Black males used no method. For unplanned events, 56 percent of White males and 71 percent of Black males reported "none." Thus, the incidence of unprotected intercourse at initiation is very high. When asked why no method was used, White males tended to state that intercourse was not planned or contraceptives were not available, confirming anecdotal reports on the high value put on spontaneity. Black males said they did not know about contraception or they or their partners were unwilling to use methods available at the time.

The Baltimore survey yielded more detailed information on contraceptive use among urban Black adolescent males (Clark, 1984). Fully four-fifths of that sample reported that they had ever used contraception and three-fifths had used a method at last coitus (a very high utilization rate). The majority of users mentioned using male methods with less than one-third employing pills. Among all sexually active males, about one-fourth had used condoms at last coitus. This compares with the earlier study of a similar population; 28 percent reported using condoms last time (Finkel, 1978).

Hogan (et al., 1985) reported a low level of contraceptive use at first intercourse among a sample of Black Chicago males, aged 13 to 19. Only 18 percent of the respondents reported use, but strong social class differentials were found: about one-third of high social class males used contraception the first time compared to 10 percent of the low social class. Use was somewhat related to career aspirations, neighborhood quality, parents' marital status and parental supervision.

Knowledge and Attitudes

*W*hen asked the time of greatest risk of pregnancy, only ten percent of boys in the Baltimore study answered correctly and one-third admitted they did not know. However, 90 percent knew a girl could get pregnant if she only has sex once. Marsiglio and Mott (1986) conducted an analysis of the National Longitudinal Survey data to measure the impact of sex education on the initiation of sexual intercourse and other behaviors. They report only eight percent of males had received sex education by age 13, 28 percent by age 16, and 52 percent by age 19. Females were more likely to have attended a course than males at all ages, and Whites, both male and female, had higher levels of attendance than Blacks or Hispanics. Thus, only about half of all young men have been exposed to a formal sex-education course. And in these courses, the subject least likely to be covered is where to obtain contraception.

It is not surprising that males have a low level of knowledge about pregnancy risk. The NLSY study showed that only 27 percent of all male respondents aged 19 to 27 could correctly answer the question about when during the menstrual cycle risk is the greatest (about two weeks after period begins). Those who had taken a sex education course did better than the others, 32 versus 22 percent, but this means two-thirds of the course takers did not know that important piece of information (Marsiglio and Mott, 1986).

In general, boys appear to know even less about contraception than girls do (Davis, 1982), although they have equal exposure to sex-education classes that include instruction in contraceptive methods (Zelnik, 1982). Despite their ignorance about the subject, boys apparently exert a strong influence on their partner's use of contraception. Young males seem particularly concerned about side effects from pills, and express fears for the health of their partners ("they'll get cancer"). Another worry often cited is fear of interference in pleasure from use of condoms and IUD's; some boys claim that they can feel the tip of the IUD (Swanson, 1984). Focus group interviews with Hispanic adolescents revealed strong objections to use of condoms because of loss of sensation and embarrassment connected with procuring them (Darabi, 1984). "Boys fear that girls will laugh at them, have second thoughts...or talk about their poor performance, if they stop to use a condom."

Boys appear to know very little about birth control, and are often misinformed about side effects and proper usage. They do not have the skills for communicating their concerns to their partners or other adults who might help them. It is ironic that they appear to exert so much control over the decision to contracept. Many studies and anecdotal reports confirm that the greatest influence on the use of contraception is the male partner.

Some two out of five boys in the Baltimore study thought condoms were too much of a hassle to use and almost half said they would be embarrassed to buy any kind of birth control in a store. However, most of these boys had positive attitudes toward birth control and thought it was a good idea to prevent pregnancy. In general, they saw the issue as a joint responsibility. Other studies have shown that adolescent males who took greater responsibility for contraception were older, more experienced with relationships, concerned about their partner's pleasure as well as their own and were opposed to risk-taking (Chilman, 1983).

One attitude revealed in a small survey of young Black rural males was a distrust of women (Kinsey, 1982). The belief that some girls want to become pregnant or have difficulty using birth control pills contributed to the assumption that women could not be trusted to adequately contracept. The study cites one 15 year old who decided to use a condom the first time because "I didn't want no kids. You see a lot of boys running around with babies—not me. It's hard to stop and think to put it on—some girls don't want you to use it, I guess 'cause they want to get pregnant."

Another theme revealed in the Kinsey (Jennifer) study was the problems connected with first use of a condom: "It felt funny; it was slippery—it's OK once you get used to using them." The author comments:

> Often such sentiments—that condom use becomes more acceptable over time—were accompanied with comments that non-users who believe that condoms detract from sex are often men who have only used condoms a few times and therefore have never been through the initial adaptation period.

Almost half of the condom users interviewed had experienced condom breakage at some time.

IV
Pregnancy:
Who Are the
Fathers?

Some young males want to sire children at early ages, particularly in communities where opportunities for self-realization or success through economic enhancement are limited (Sullivan, 1985). One hears anecdotes about boys who brag about impregnating large numbers of neighborhood girls. Teenage mothers often say, "I gave him his baby because that's what he wanted." In one study of low-income Black youngsters in Washington, over two-thirds of the boys expected to father a baby out-of-wedlock, a higher proportion than among girls (McAdoo, 1985). Other studies have confirmed that out-of-wedlock teenage fatherhood is intergenerational (e.g., teen fathers were born when *their* fathers were teens), following the patterns of teenage motherhood.

We do not know how many teenaged fathers there are each year because many birth certificates do not contain information about the age of the father. Of the 479,647 births to teenage girls (19 or under) in 1984, only 19 percent were fathered by males the same age, 35 percent by fathers aged 20 to 24, 7 percent to fathers aged 25 to 29, and 37 percent were born to fathers whose ages were not stated (the remaining two percent were fathers 30 and over) (National Center for Health Statistics, 1986). (For those who collect odd facts, 206 of the fathers of teenaged girls' babies were aged 50 and over). Father's age is less often stated when the birth is out-of-wedlock.

In 1984, only 89,000 boys under the age of 20 were identified as fathers. The Vital Statistics data confirm the anecdotal evidence that teenage girls are impregnated by boys several years older than they are (assuming that the missing data are distributed equally with the available data). Age specific fertility rates by sex and race demonstrate these differences (Table 4). In 1984 for White 15 to 19 year olds, the fertility rate was 14.8 per 1,000 for fathers and 44.6 per 1,000 for mothers while for Blacks, the comparable rates were 41.0 and 95.7. Black teen males are three times as likely as White teen males to be fathers, but Black teen males are less than half as likely as Black females to become parents during a year (at least according to *reported* paternity). For White teenagers, the sex differential is even greater: girls were three times as likely as boys to become parents.

Table 4
Birth Rates for Fathers and Mothers Age 15-19 by Race, 1970-1984
(Live Births per 1,000 Men and Women)

	White		Black	
	Father	Mother	Father	Mother
1984	14.8	44.6	41.0	95.7
1980	15.2	44.7	40.4	100.0
1975	17.1	46.4	45.0	111.8
1970	21.0	57.4	58.7	147.7
# change	-7.1	-14.9	-17.7	-52.0
% change	-33.8%	-26.0%	-30.2%	-35.2%

Source: National Center for Health Statistics, 1986

In an analysis of the National Longitudinal Survey of Youth (NLSY), Marsiglio (1987) identified young men who reported (when they were aged 20 to 27) that they had become fathers while teenagers. Almost seven percent said they had experienced fatherhood. Blacks and Hispanics showed higher rates (15 and 11 percent respectively). This study also presents separate rates for poor and non-poor Whites. The disadvantaged White males reported significantly higher fertility rates (12 percent) than non-poor Whites (5 percent), levels of early paternity similar to minority-group males. Amongst all the teen fathers, over 80 percent had children before marriage. However, 36 percent of Hispanics and 25 percent of White males (with no differences related to poverty) said the births were conceived post-marriage compared to only four percent of the Black males.

Since 1970, all adolescent fertility rates have dropped (Table 4), and most significantly among Black females. All of these rates for males must be considered in the context of changes in out-of-wedlock birth rates which have been rapidly increasing among White teens. This could have the effect of repressing the reported White male paternity rate.

An examination of these data about male fertility rates and sexual activity point toward a paradoxical situation. Turning to the female side of the equation, we know that of the five million sexually active girls under the age of 19, approximately 20 percent (one million) get pregnant in a year. Looking at the seven-million sexually active boys under the age of 19, we can account for only 89,000 births. Assuming that half the unknown fathers were teens, we could add another 88,000, making 177,000 teen fathers. Even if all the 400,000 abortions that occur to teen girls were conceived with teen boys, this would imply only about 600,000 pregnancies attributable to those seven million sexually active males, a pregnancy rate of about 8.6 percent. If teen males start having sexual relations earlier, know less about contraception, use less contraception than females, and are more casual in their relationships, why should they have lower pregnancy rates than females?

One explanation could be that males report much higher rates of sexual activity than actually occur. Another could be girls with multiple partners. Other theories are welcome.

V
Male
Involvement
Programs

*W*hen male involvement programs are discussed, the activity that comes to mind is most likely condom distribution. Under the guise of the male involvement initiative, a whole range of programs has been developed, but the primary *male* activity centers around distributing condoms. Programs called outreach, education, motivation, peer involvement and advocacy all have some element of method provision. However, there are a few clinic based programs rooted in a strong belief that males are as entitled to the full range of the medical model as females. In a few birth control clinics, males may receive physical examinations, but most male clinic users are not adolescents. More typically, comprehensive health services in community centers or schools may provide contraception to males as well as females.

It is not easy to sort out the different types of male programs; there is clearly an overlap between them. Nevertheless, the discussion that follows attempts to summarize a number of different approaches and the little that is known about their strong and weak points. The approaches include sex education, decision making and life planning, parent involvement, teen peer advocates, teen theater, condom distribution, male outreach programs, clinic-based programs, comprehensive health and social services, school-based clinics, services that "add on" pregnancy prevention, AIDS prevention and youth-serving organizations' efforts.

Sex Education

*I*t is difficult to report how many teen males have had access to sex education courses. Reports from individuals yield much lower rates than reports from school systems. As mentioned above, Marsiglio and Mott (1986) estimated that around 50 percent of teen males had attended a course. A survey of 13 to 19 year old males conducted by the Harris Poll (1986) shows about the same level, but differentiates between comprehensive and noncomprehensive courses. Only one third of the boys reported they had received a comprehensive course including information about where to get birth control. Half of those who had received sex education did so in only one grade, and only one third had a separate course in sex education (rather than combined with some other course).

According to the report of the National Academy of Sciences, "sex education in schools is burgeoning" (Hayes, 1987). They cite a 1982 survey of school districts that showed fully three-quarters provided some sex education in their junior and senior high schools, and two-thirds in elementary schools.

It has been well documented that sex education may be expected to increase knowledge and change attitudes but not have a large effect on behavior (Kirby, 1983). In addition to the NLSY study cited above, there are several small studies showing that boys who had sex education were slightly more knowledgeable than those who didn't (Toronto, 1982) and one study showed that males scoring the highest on knowledge tests were the most interested in gaining additional knowledge. Anecdotal reports suggest that sex education as it is currently offered to inner-city boys does not take. While many boys are taught about contraception in school, the information either comes too late or is not presented in a form that makes it salient to the boys.

Evidence abounds that boys are very interested in learning about sex and responsive to the idea of male involvement. Many of the materials used to teach boys are not developmentally appropriate. For inner-city youth, the curricula often suffer from a middle-class White bias. Many boys have difficulty reading, a requirement in most courses. Sex education teachers are most often females and rarely trained to deal with gender and cultural differences and developmental issues.

Whatever is or is not going on in school, boys rely more on other sources for information about sex. Many studies document the strong influence of peers in this knowledge domain. In one study, Davis (1982) shows that young males rely heavily on their friends for information and are much less likely than young females to talk to parents. In addition to peers, books, magazines, movies, teachers and lastly parents were cited as a source of sexual data. The Harris poll (1986) found greater reliance on parents for information as well as courses and teachers. Medical personnel and clinics were least mentioned as a source. In any case, misinformation is widely circulated through the peer grape vine and therefore it is not surprising that boys know so little. They think they know a great deal but what they know is largely incorrect.

Decision Making and Life Planning

*I*n recent years, there has been an increasing recognition that sex education is not a potent enough intervention to make a large impact on teenage pregnancy rates. It has become increasingly clear that the rationale for delaying parenthood must be interrelated with making decisions about life goals and gaining an understanding that achievement of goals would be frustrated by early parenthood. This message is much clearer for girls than for boys since in many cases, boys' lives are not affected by becoming fathers. Nevertheless, the materials used in these approaches are useful for boys for career planning, decision making and consciousness raising.

The Life Planning curriculum developed by the Center for Population Options is initiated through a wide range of youth serving organizations within a community whose staffs are trained by CPO consultants to work with their students and/or clients to use this vocational guidance *cum* family planning educational program. Preliminary results from El Paso show a high degree of community participation and very positive reactions from the adolescents who went through the course.

A similar intervention has been designed by the Girls Clubs of Santa Barbara. *Choices* is a workbook that is used for a full term course in 10th grade, incorporating exercises dealing with vocational choice, family design and pregnancy prevention. *Choices* has been rewritten for males; the result is called *Challenges*. *Choices* is being evaluated to measure impact on the girls who took the course. No plans have been announced to evaluate the male version.

The life planning curriculum has been modified to better meet the needs of low-income and minority youngsters. Public/Private Ventures has incorporated this concept into the STEP (Summer Training and Education Program) demonstration projects, combining life planning education with school remediation and job placement and training (see comprehensive programs, below). This approach is also being used in several of the projects of the Urban Middle Schools Adolescent Pregnancy Prevention Program (UMSAP). All of these eight middle-school programs include boys, and in Boston, Los Angeles and Oakland, life planning curricula have been adapted to the special needs of the target population.

The Teen Intervention Project (TIP) was created in Atlanta schools as part of the UMSAP program to improve decision-making skills of sixth and seventh grade males. This

44

is implemented through group sessions in school and individual mentoring in conjunction with the Alpha Phi Alpha fraternity. A full-time coordinator works with a core support team in the participating schools to raise consciousness, expedite referrals and stimulate activities. Site visitors have observed the success of the one-on-one approach to interest boys in this project. Another approach to decision making involves training youngsters in communication to improve interpersonal skills, a technique developed by Steven Schinke (Blythe, 1981). Using very small samples of high school students, the researchers documented a greater commitment to postponing pregnancy and better use of birth control among participants than among a control group. Some experts in adolescent development believe that this technique has the highest potential for helping young people (Chilman, 1985).

There is growing recognition that early sexual initiation is not an isolated act. The Problem Behavior theory suggests a syndrome of acting out in school, early substance abuse, truancy, delinquency and early intercourse. Analysis of the predictors of these behaviors showed many common attributes: low academic achievement, absence of parental supervision, lack of resistance to peer pressures and non-conformity (Dryfoos, 1987). These findings can help shape more effective interventions. A number of curricula developed for prevention of smoking are now being adapted for broader use, to change social behavior in general. The works of Gilbert Botvin (1986), Schinke and others point toward the importance of teaching social skills, resistance strategies and other behavioral mechanisms that may help young people deal with the many pressures they face.

Computer games that force decisions on life goals and paths to achieve these goals have been developed. The Body Awareness Network Project (Barny) of the University of Wisconsin has circulated a tape cassette that is popular with young males. A film modeled after a TV game show has been produced by the Ounce of Prevention Fund. It takes a young couple through decision making steps that help them avoid early unplanned parenthood and gain career choices.

Another type of intervention that focuses on teaching the consequences of parenthood places young boys in direct contact with infants and children. Boys are recruited to work or act as volunteers in day care centers.

These types of interventions are difficult to evaluate but if we apply the common sense test, they appear to be reasonable programs to introduce to younger boys and girls around fifth or sixth grade. Since career goals can only be achieved if academic programs are lined up to facilitate the goals, the decision should be discussed at an early age. Children who get tracked into nonacademic courses have little chance of breaking out of that mold when they get to high school (if they get to high school). Perhaps the most important impact a Life Planning curriculum could have is to force an institutional response and require schools to make educational components available that would insure life plans could be implemented. Without that assurance, many of these decision-making models leave a youngster with a lot of aspiration but no real possibility for making it.

Parent Involvement

*F*ather-son workshops are being offered by Planned Parenthood in Seattle. Aimed at boys aged 10 to 12, classes discuss issues related to puberty and work to open up parent-child communication. Boys are also taught self-examination of the testes.

At one time, the Austin, Texas Planned Parenthood ran father-son workshops as part of a broad male involvement program. A program in St. Joseph, Missouri, brings fathers and sons together for six weekly classes covering a wide range of sexuality and pregnancy issues. Communication skills, values clarification and decision-making skills are emphasized. A manual describing the curriculum is available. This program has been evaluated showing gains in knowledge among the students and increased parent-child communication. One of the important components of its success is the wide base of support; the Family Life Center has elicited cosponsorship from local schools, PTA's, YMCA's, churches and other youth organizations.

A number of church groups have developed curricula that are used in parent seminars, parent-child workshops and weekend family retreats, such as Catholic Charities, National Council of Churches and the Methodist Church.

In theory, working with parents to educate their children about sexual issues is an excellent idea. In practice, it is difficult to recruit parents, particularly in low-income areas. According to Phillip Coltoff, Executive Director of Children's Aid Society of New York City, "agencies serving youth...in poverty [should] integrate sexuality education...into a broader life skills program intended to increase information, enhance self-esteem, and build goal-setting skills" (CPO, undated). He suggests programs be brought *into* poverty neighborhoods rather than expecting parents to travel.

Teen Peer Advocate Programs

A survey of fifty teen peer advocate programs around the country revealed that only a few were either male-focused or included a male outreach component (Talbot, 1982). Peer advocate programs are defined as interventions in which teenagers fill the role of educator or counselor of other teens, outreach person or resource worker in schools or communities and/or advisor in the design of programs for teens. The theory is that teens may be more effective than adults at communicating with their peers. Male programs are directed at promoting male responsibility through special educational approaches about condom use, STDs, fatherhood and roles in pregnancy prevention. Strategies mentioned include informal street contact, school and community presentations, condom distribution and one-on-one contact in other community agencies.

The study concluded that it was important for teen peer advocate programs to recruit males to advocacy positions. Males could be utilized in roles such as condom distribution where they might be more effective than females, given the embarrassment factor associated with condoms. However, the survey found it was difficult to recruit males for these positions, just as it was difficult to get males to attend family planning clinics.

A recent group discussion with male involvement workers in an urban community centered on the difficulties encountered when working in a disorganized, dangerous inner-city setting. The young males, whose job it was to convince their younger peers to use condoms and/or come to the local family planning clinic, reported the low priority given to the problem of teenage pregnancy in light of high crime rates and massive unemployment. As they said, the bottom line was getting people jobs, and that's what kids wanted to talk about. They also described the openness with which drugs and gambling were treated, even in front of the schools. The teen male advocates employed in this program expressed great appreciation for having been selected, trained and given important tasks to do, even though they were skeptical about their impact on their peers.

In general, peer programs seem to have a large effect on participants and to raise agency awareness about the importance of involving clinics in the design of interventions. The effect of these programs on reaching peers is questionable, especially for young males. This may reflect the need among young boys for more authoritative role models than other boys.

Teen Theater

A very popular attraction that involves young males in pregnancy prevention is teen theater. Groups have sprung up around the country, organized by Planned Parenthood affiliates or other family planning agencies, that recruit 10 to 20 young people who form a troupe of players. Presentations are generally written by the group: they are the actors and, following performances, they often serve as peer communicators or counselors.

One of the first groups operated out of Metropolitan Hospital in New York. A typical performance for a large professional audience resulted in meaningful discussion between the actors and the audience regarding parent-child relationships, permissiveness, suicide, condom use, dating and other relevant topics. This particular audience was deeply moved by the experience and felt the process was unusually effective at stimulating an interchange.

Observing another teen theater group performing for a private school ninth grade group and their parents revealed less open communication, few questions and some uncomfortableness on the part of the parents. The general approach of the players was to open a question through dramatic skits and leave the resolution of the problem to the audience. Here the questions had to do with whether or not a girl should have an abortion, whether a boy should try drugs in order to keep up with his peers, and similar human predicaments.

In a number of communities, these Teen Theater groups have been invited into schools to perform and often they bring up controversial subjects that are not usually allowed on the premises. In one otherwise restrictive school system, the theater group performs in conjunction with a school health fair and the messages during the performance are tied with prevention messages from health agencies participating in the fair. This group has been highly rated by students in the school and invitations are increasing over time.

Participation in a theater group requires large time commitment from the boys and girls selected. They usually meet with a program director three or four times a week in addition to their performances, often on weekends. As with peer advocates, the impact on the participants is large. Many report their "lives have been turned around." A number of the participants are interested in becoming professional actors; others get caught up in the counseling aspects of the experience.

Condom Distribution

*I*nterventions directed toward condom distribution are more strictly male involvement programs than those considered so far. Prior to the wide scale distribution of contraceptive pills through family planning delivery system, condoms were the method of choice among U.S. families. Most American boys grew up with condoms in their wallets, even if they never had the opportunity to use them. According to Scales, condom sales hit an all-time low in 1970 which he attributes to the assumption by males that all females were protected because they had pills and IUDs. As he points out, birth control had become a "women's issue" and men began to think of condoms as old-fashioned and unattractive (Scales, 1982). During this period, condoms got their "bum rap": it was widely believed that condoms interfered with sexual pleasure.

Only recently, many professionals interested in pregnancy prevention have begun to promote condom use, recognizing that especially among teens, the gap between first intercourse and first contraception often stretches beyond a year, a year in which young girls are at very high risk of unintended pregnancy. A few staunch advocates of condom distribution have been conducting isolated programs over the years. However, these efforts have not resulted in program models that have been replicated around the country. Now the threat of AIDS has brought condoms out of the closet. Not a day passes when we don't hear about safe sex and new controversies relating to AIDS education, condom advertising and related issues. But we still have little data on how to develop programs.

One of the best documented condom distribution programs took place in the late 1960's in North Carolina (the University of North Carolina population program spawned a number of condom advocates) (Arnold, 1973). The project distributed condoms through an anti-poverty agency summer youth program, using male outreach workers who organized condom depots in pool halls, barber shops, a restaurant and a grocery store. This program was carefully evaluated. A study of program operations found: more condoms were distributed during the week than on weekends; consumers tended to use distribution sites near where they lived; the demand did not place a burden on the shopkeepers (average of 7.5 young men per day); and the type of shop did not make any difference. Users were found to be similar to the population in the target area. In a survey that tracked condom usage over the course of a year, 69 to 81 percent of the respondents reported they had used a condom at their last intercourse.

Finally, Arnold reports that the fertility rate of Black women aged 10 to 19 residing in the target area declined 19 percent compared to other parts of the county where no decline was observed.

In the early 1970's, the South Carolina Health Department sent a health educator (on his motorcycle) around to pool halls, factories and bars, places where men would congregate (Mescia, 1973). He stressed the importance of condoms in VD prevention and talked to the clients "man-to-man" about the importance of birth control. About 2,500 young men were seen over a two-year period. Because of the success of the program (as measured by numbers of clients), the Health Department hoped to launch a statewide program for male involvement, using male outreach workers to instruct men in basic reproductive facts, increase men's understanding of effective female methods such as pills and IUDs, distribute condoms, counsel about vasectomies and other medical and social needs and check for VD symptoms. (This statewide initiative was never funded.)

The Maryland State Health Department currently leads the country in condom distribution with its exemplary Three-for-Free program. In 1988, over half-a-million condoms will be handed out in 170 sites located in 22 of the state's 23 counties. The number of condoms distributed increased 10 fold by the second year of operation. Condoms are distributed in bags in quantities of 3 to 15 along with a simple easy-to-read pamphlet on correct condom use. Emphasis was placed on permitting individuals to pick up condoms anonymously, without requiring any kind of registration, counseling or discussion. The staff believe this kind of open, non-hassle distribution system increases utilization.

The program was designed and implemented by Sam Clark and Therese McCluskey. Sponsors include 19 of the 23 county health departments, social service agencies, university health centers, community clinics and the Baltimore City Health Department. Many agencies have multiple sites. Sponsors must agree to put condoms and pamphlets in an accessible place that is open most of the time, to monitor the number taken, and to *not* ask any questions of the users. Attractive posters are available, and sponsors are assisted to prepare press releases and other outreach.

Sam Clark feels the Three-for-Free program "serves as a vehicle for raising awareness concerning the appropriateness of condoms and men's involvement in family planning and STD prevention. Condoms are so cheap that they cost no more than the brochures to be distributed with them" (Clark, 1988). As he points out, half-a-million condoms at five cents each ($25,000) costs less than caring for one person with AIDS for a year. He estimates the total cost to the state for a year is $40,000. The Maryland Department of Health expects to continue to expand the Three-for-Free program to new sites, especially in areas perceived to be at high risk for unplanned pregnancies and sexually transmitted diseases.

One example of a Three-for-Free distribution site is the Boy's Club in Hagerstown, Maryland. A health educator presents films and other educational materials along with free condoms. Users who were queried liked the films and particularly liked being able to get condoms at the Boy's Club. In a follow-up survey, it was reported that boys were glad to be able to get condoms in places where they socialized and planned their evenings, where they could prepare themselves for "tonight" (Kinsey, 1982).

Condom distribution programs can be organized in many different kinds of locations.

As mentioned above, barber shops and pool halls were popular sites in more rural areas. More recent programs appear to be located in recreational centers, sports areas or on the streets. Other sites include industrial places, labor unions, schools, abortion clinics, VD clinics, hospital outpatient services and emergency rooms, and just about anywhere. In England, barber shops sell one third of all condoms. In some communities, free standing store fronts have been used for disseminating literature, counseling and condom distribution. The Rubber Tree in Seattle, Washington is a prototype of such a program. A new program will be launched in Oakland using pharmacies to sell condoms at reduced prices, stimulating sales through advertising and handing out coupons for free samples.

One approach used by condom advocates has been the organization of *National Condom Week,* started by pharmacies in California; rubber discos and rallies are held all over the country around Valentine's Day. Planned Parenthood of Washington, D.C. at one time celebrated the occasion with a major event in which condoms were inflated, decorated and let loose over the nation's capitol. The event was controversial enough to be cited by conservative legislators as an example of Title X excesses and Planned Parenthood has stopped that activity.

Argument will continue about the effectiveness of condom distribution programs in pregnancy prevention. The positive arguments are:

- Condoms are low cost.
- They can be delivered outside the medical care system; highly trained medical personnel are not necessary.
- Used properly, they are relatively effective (more effective than diaphragms).
- No medical or health risks are associated with their use.
- Condoms can be stored easily and carried around inconspicuously.
- Use of condoms prevents STDs.
- Use of condoms with spermicides may prevent AIDS.

The negative arguments are:

- The primary source of condoms is drug stores (still) and it is embarrassing to ask for them under those circumstances.
- Condoms are associated with VD and AIDS.
- They are believed to decrease the sensation of sexual experience.
- They are believed to be ineffective; females place little confidence in them.
- The price of condoms in retail stores is relatively high compared to the actual cost.
- There is a lack of advertising and packaging so most males are not even aware of the benefits of condoms.

The greatest barrier to use by teenagers is probably the condom's bad reputation for decreasing sexual satisfaction. To gain acceptance for the condom might require innovative educational and motivational approaches, including the use of role models and authority figures who attest to the pleasure that condom use might bring (like delayed ejaculation and protection from AIDS). Adult males might be especially well suited for this kind of outreach.

Evaluation of condom programs is impossible in most communities because of the large number of other influences on fertility rates (that were not evident in the early North Carolina

51

days). One problem is the substitution effect. If girls give up using pills as boys begin using condoms, the pregnancy rate could increase. Acceptance of packages of condoms does not necessarily mean they will be used consistently, or ever. In some programs, boys took large numbers of condoms to impress their peers and in other cases, it was suspected that the packages were sold.

Male Outreach and Media Programs

*N*ot all outreach programs concentrate on condom distribution. Many male involvement efforts are largely educational or motivational. A typical outreach program is attached to a Planned Parenthood affiliate or other Title X grantee (health department, hospital or poverty agency); the agency hires several young males to work where other young males congregate. Sites are generally community centers, recreational areas, schools and the streets. In one effort, films are shown in a community center, followed by discussion about sexual roles and responsibilities.

Outreach programs appear to be designed with attention to target populations. In an area with many Hispanic families, outreach workers are also Hispanic and are trained to be sensitive to the need of Hispanic males to feel they are in control of their partners' sexual behavior. Educational materials have been developed to help these men to understand birth control and to encourage their wives to use family planning clinics. In an inner-city program, Black young men have been recruited and trained to work with their peers on the streets to convince them to come to clinics for condoms and information.

One innovative approach makes video tapes of boys playing basketball and then invites them to the Young Men's Clinic at Columbia/Presbyterian Medical Center to view the tapes (Armstrong, 1988). The "commercials" are prevention messages delivered by the staff to the participants. Medical students serve as volunteer counselors (and role models) and talk to the young men about sexuality issues and career possibilities. At the clinic, young men may obtain condoms and receive instruction on first aid and pregnancy prevention. T-shirts and baseball caps are presented to attendees. Armstrong stresses the importance of involving a network of adult gatekeepers who refer boys to the clinic.

The primary purpose of most male outreach programs is educational as differentiated from peer advocacy programs where the goal is more typically clinic recruitment. One school based campaign in Delaware trains journalism teachers and guidance counselors who work with students in their schools. They encourage students to write articles and presentations about male involvement in pregnancy prevention for school newspapers, drama clubs and other media.

The Austin, Texas Planned Parenthood, some years ago, developed one of the most comprehensive male involvement programs in the country. Much of the effort of its health education staff was directed toward the local schools including presentations in after-school sessions with the high school football team and coaches (Schoot, 1981). Materials such as posters, brochures and other items that began with a positive approach (passing up guilt-inducing messages or other negative tactics) were produced. The emphasis was on responsibility and caring, suggesting that gentle, sensitive, compassionate traits are just as masculine as being tough or macho.

Another male outreach program was specifically designed to meet the needs of the community, based on findings of a local needs assessment survey. Planned Parenthood of Southeastern Pennsylvania operates Project MARCH (Men Acting Responsibly for Contraception and Health), a community education effort that relies heavily on marketing services and concepts through brochures, fliers and wallet cards. Although the initial idea was to bring young men into the clinic for medical services, the program rapidly shifted to community education and public awareness when it became clear that adolescent males were reluctant to present themselves at Planned Parenthood. The male health educators respond to requests from residential centers, juvenile homes and Big Brothers for presentations regarding male sexuality and health. The program also trains clinicians to treat males. Earnest Peacock, MARCH health educator, reports heavy demand and considerable media coverage for this "man-to-man" rap session approach.

The use of media figures prominently in the new wave of male outreach programs. The National Urban League launched a media campaign aimed at young Black males—"You don't have to be a father to be a brother"—presented in three posters and a 60 second radio spot. Local affiliates have been encouraged to add their own tag to encourage young males to come to the Urban League offices to talk about pregnancy prevention.

In Portland, Maine, the Males Preventing Pregnancy program has developed a multimedia campaign using posters, bus cards and TV public service announcements. A booklet, "Becoming a Teenage Father is no Joke," describes Maine's paternity laws. A large scale campaign in central Ohio proclaims, "find out the facts of life before experience becomes the worst teacher," and uses posters and corresponding television spots to direct young boys and girls to a teenage hotline. About 15 percent of the hotline callers are males. The Planned Parenthood affiliate that operates the hotline attributes a decrease in teen fertility to the availability of the hotline and its impact on increased clinic utilization by young men. One outreach program features a half hour weekly talk show on the leading local rock station. An increase in clinic utilization has been attributed to the show's success and its youthful host's ability to deal with sensitive questions and his willingness to directly refer callers to specialized agencies for more information.

Outreach covers a multitude of approaches carried out in many different locations. Scales mentions a number of other outreach methods that have been used to provide an educational component for males: workshops on sexuality offered at high schools, community talks, handing out frisbees and matchbooks with printed messages, T-shirt giveaways, and ads in yearbooks and the mass transit. Another form of outreach to boys utilizes adult volunteers who act as "surrogate" parents in one-on-one relationships. Several national Black fraternities and church groups have organized such programs that offer role models, mentoring and recreation.

Documentation of outreach efforts from the Teen Father Collaborative provides useful insights into the difficulties of involving males in programs. "Unlike young women, young men do not come into social programs on their own...they require a great deal of encouragement before they will investigate or utilize available services" (Sanders and Rosen, 1987). About one third of the clients in the Teen Father programs were brought in by their female partners, some by friends after the programs were established, but most by aggressive recruitment. The outreach workers had to go into target communities and approach young men on a one-to-one basis. Other outreach was conducted in school presentations, through school guidance departments and the media.

Family Planning Clinic-based Programs for Males

*C*urrently, there are four to five thousand family planning clinics operating in the United States. However, federal policies discourage clinics that receive public funding through Title X (Family Planning and Population Research Act) from using their resources to serve males. Before 1982, clinics could count males as patients in their aggregate caseloads. At that time, less than one-half percent of all family planning users were males. Thus, even when the clinics were encouraged to enroll males, only about 20,000 young men obtained family planning services including physical examination and instruction in methods. However, many more men entered the clinics with their partners, attended counseling sessions and received publications.

A survey of 35 family planning agencies in 1984 showed that services for males were available in every one of the responding clinics (Swanson and Forrest, 1987). However, very few of the clients were males; 21 of the 31 respondents providing utilization data said 100 percent of their clients were female, and the remainder reported low numbers of males obtaining medical services. The most typical transaction involved male partners in education/counseling sessions. Most agencies had pamphlets and films that dealt with male issues and about half had male staff members, mostly physicians and/or administrators.

Barriers to the provision of male services included: limited resources, negative staff attitudes, and lack of staff training and experience. Some agencies commented that previous efforts to involve males had elicited poor responses. Others reported funding disapprovals and plans to decrease whatever male services they were currently providing. Swanson and Forrest see these survey results as indicating "a widespread discrepancy between the nominal offering of services and their actual utilization, a 'phantom services' phenomenon."

Levine and Thornton (1985) conducted a similar survey of 14 family planning agencies in one urban area. Their findings confirm the previous report: very little action, no funds for male services, few male staff members, and limited interest in beefing up male programs. Only two of the programs had policies that routinely encouraged female patients to bring along their partners. Several sites restricted registration to females (in one such site, a successful condom distribution program for young males had to be terminated because they were not official patients). Levine summarizes the situation: "The programs simply reflect

56

society at large by basing their services on the prevailing beliefs that male teenagers are not interested in being sexually responsible, using birth control, or caring about their partners."

Experience in the Teen Father Collaborative is applicable to other male involvement programs. Lack of success was attributed to agency ambivalence about working with males, typically generated by an administrator who was not fully committed to the concept. Successful approaches to males were made by aggressive, street smart counselors, characterized as men aged 20 to 30, of the same ethnic/cultural background as the potential clients. Staff had to be equipped to deal with clients' suspicions about the motives of the program, and to handle clients' irresponsibility when it came to issues like keeping appointments (Sanders and Rosen, 1987).

Despite the difficulties encountered, a few family planning agencies have developed comprehensive male programs. The Male's Place appears to have all the earmarks of success.

The Male's Place is one of the few male programs operated by a local health department (Graham, 1988). It is an excellent example of a comprehensive program that has been able to attract young males for both educational and medical services. The Mecklenburg County Health Department funds special weekly sessions in the Charlotte, North Carolina, family planning clinic, providing free family planning, medical counseling and educational services to males aged 15 to 24. This program was started in 1981 with a Title X (Family Planning) grant. When those funds were cut off, the Health Department assumed fiscal responsibility.

Stanley Graham, the program administrator, reports that in 1987 more than 300 young men received medical examinations in this facility. Every male patient must attend an educational class that discusses life choices, reproductive health, venereal diseases and contraception and teaches how to conduct self-testes examinations. A special slide presentation has been prepared for educational purposes. A doctor performs a comprehensive physical examination, tests for sickle cell and STD, and does other health screening. At an exit interview, every male patient is offered condoms. Transportation to clinics is provided. In addition, anyone can come into the health department clinic at any time to obtain condoms. Graham says that the clinic sessions are over-crowded and the condom distribution is being utilized "in the thousands."

Community education is a high priority for the Male's Place. In 1987, about 7,000 young males were contacted through outreach by male educators. Mobile clinical screenings are conducted in prisons, Boys Clubs, church centers and schools; teenage sexuality workshops that also include information about general health, values and substance abuse are presented in many locations; posters, "urinal stickers," public service announcements and other intensive media approaches are widely used. Two male health educators spend time rapping with young men in pool halls, locker rooms, bars and nightclubs, game rooms, basketball courts, and other informal meeting places.

The success of this male improvement program may be attributable to the working relationships established by the Male's Place staff with other community agencies, including Planned Parenthood, neighborhood centers, the local housing authority, parks and recreation, Boys Clubs, Department of Corrections, churches and parent groups. Outreach has been concentrated on high risk young men, through satellite workshops/rap sessions and informal contacts.

The Male's Place is part of an extensive teen pregnancy prevention program launched by the Mecklenburg County Health Department. This effort has received national recognition; the National Association of Counties presented a County Achievement Award in 1987 for their "Teen Fest '86" Rap Contest/Disco. This was a collaborative community-wide event involving 13 to 19 year olds in a contest for cash prizes for a rapping contest on the subject of teenage pregnancy.

Planned Parenthood of Western Michigan also operates a comprehensive male involvement program (Men's Reproductive Health, 1988). One component concentrates on serving partners of female clients. When women call for an appointment, they are encouraged to bring their partners. Men receive free information packets including four sample condoms. They are encouraged to participate in their partners' educational sessions and to buy condoms at low prices. Steve Creamer, program director, reports significant increases in male attendance at clinic and condom purchases. Community education programs range from workshops for individual agencies to a series of regional conferences on male involvement.

Using a grant from an early Title X initiative (1978), the Austin (Texas) Planned Parenthood claimed early success in involving males in many aspects of its service components: male partners accompanied clients through all stages of the contraceptive visit including the physical exam; vasectomy surgery was more heavily utilized; and more than 80,000 condoms were distributed from the "condom barrel" over a three year period (Schott, 1981). These changes were attributed to the addition of six full-time male employees to a staff of twenty-two; the development of educational materials and posters to facilitate dialogue about men's role; and a general consciousness-raising within the affiliate and by the affiliate out in the community. (This program is no longer in operation.)

One male involvement program that met with little success was organized in Pittsburgh (Middleman, 1972), "Attendance was consistently low even when high-key publicity was employed." None of the users were under 18 and only 10 percent were under 20. Vasectomy counseling and referral were the most sought after services.

An analysis of the failure of the men's clinic of the San Francisco District Health Center Number 4 after six years of operation lends more fuel to the controversy over the efficacy of using family planning clinics as the base for male involvement programs (Gordon, 1984). The concept for this clinic grew out of the activism of the early 1970's that thrust forward free-standing family planning clinics. "The program was inspired by a wide range of social research findings, many of them in the international field, illustrating the importance of involving men, if family planning programs were to be successful." This pilot men's clinic was comprehensive, including health education, sex counseling, contraceptive services, free physical checkups (including screening for high blood pressure, anemia, diabetes, syphilis and gonorrhea), and STD treatment. Patients were given up to two dozen condoms on a first visit.

Initially, about a third of male patients came for counseling only, seeking information on birth control methods and side effects, sexual problems, vasectomy and other subjects. However, as the clinic "aged," patients appeared to be less interested in counseling and more interested in medical treatment. Outreach efforts were concentrated on teenagers through presentations in schools and distribution of materials.

The agency had an interest in evaluation and was able to document utilization. There were about 1,200 visits per year at the men's clinic; less than 20 percent were teenagers.

Throughout the program's history, according to Gordon, there was a lack of consensus about priorities, with a competition between medical services on the one hand and educational (motivational) services on the other. While the clinic staff was committed to the idea that men should be more involved in the couple's family planning decisions, the service statistics showed that what men wanted from the clinic was primarily job physicals and free condoms. As time went on, the clinic increasingly attracted homosexual patients (as many as 60 percent of the caseload). This development further divided the staff about the efficacy of offering separate reproductive health services as compared to incorporating such services into the primary health care system. By the end of 1979, priority was shifted to educational services "as the staff began to understand the limitations of a medical model as a way of involving men, particularly adolescents, in family planning."

The article mentions a number of staffing and funding problems: integrating male staff into a female-run program; training, recruiting and keeping male staff-members; lack of male staff continuity; and annual competition for scarce financial resources. As a final blow, a researcher found that among a sample of male clients, most would have preferred to speak to a woman about family planning.

> On the basis of this experience, the authors question the need for clinic-based male involvement programs. Given the fact that withdrawal needs no program services, that the condom is already widely available...and that most vasectomies are performed by private physicians, it is difficult to know what precise role can be played by the organized family planning movement in the delivery of male-oriented birth control methods.

Gordon et al. believe males can be involved in the decision-making process through public health education campaigns, increased distribution of condoms and promotion of vasectomies. However, if a medical male contraceptive becomes available, the authors believe men will become enthusiastic clinic patients.

Research yielded few examples of successful adolescent male programs based in traditional family planning clinics. This does not mean that such programs do not exist, but the weight of the experience suggests that despite enormous efforts in program development, most clinics eventually phase out the male involvement program. Budget crunches are a major reason. The 1981 Title X budget reductions required staff cutbacks. Male staff went first (last hired, first fired). Low utilization is another explanation. Apparently males (especially adolescents) do not want to go to women-oriented clinics. Many youngsters distrust institutional settings because they are required to provide too much information about themselves in order to obtain attention from the staff. Large agencies offering vasectomies at low cost have no shortage of male customers, but sterilization services are clearly not the solution to the problem of male involvement during the teen years. While there have been reported incidents of under-age sterilization among teenaged girls, no comparable situations have been reported for teenage boys.

Comprehensive Health and Social Services

*A*s the scope of family planning clinics enlarge, many cease to be called by that name and present themselves as primary health care. There is some evidence that the comprehensive services model is more successful at attracting males than the female-oriented birth control model, for reasons discussed in the previous section. Family Health Services, Inc. of Bellafonte, Pennsylvania, is a good example of this approach. According to Walter Klausmeier, the agency's director, the private non-profit project is a delegate of the Family Planning Council of Central Pennsylvania (the Title X grantee) and offers family planning, STD treatment, and general health care to a diverse population. Men come to the clinic for general physical examinations, STD screening and treatment, condom distribution, and pre-marital examinations. Recently HIV screening has been added to the roster of services. No special outreach is directed toward adolescents but the program is advertised widely through high school yearbooks, sports programs and television (using Cable TV for ads about STDs). Services for teenage males are subsidized by Title XX social services contracts (used frequently in Pennsylvania for family planning) and EPSDT, which covers physical exams up to age 21.

This program served 1,125 males in 1987, 25 percent of the total caseload. Most of these men are not teenagers. Klausmeier attributes the success of the program to the agency's philosophy that services for males should be integrated into a general health care system. Having a wide range of offerings protects confidentiality and anonymity, particularly in an agency with an active STD program. Each patient spends time with a nurse practitioner or physician for diagnosis, treatment and counseling, very much like a doctor's office. For older men, payment is collected on a sliding scale. Appropriate staff training and advertising on TV are very important program components for serving males, according to Klausmeier; in addition, he would like to see more effective sex education carried out in home, school and church (very important in a rural area) and wider access to condoms through vending machines.

The Chattanooga-Hamilton County Health Department is operating a three-year pilot project to involve men attending the health department's STD clinic in family planning. A large number of men have enrolled in the program, receiving reproductive health screening and condoms. However, even when services for males are provided in a comprehensive health setting, the users are more likely to be older men. This suggests that the best way to reach teenagers is to bring services to them, an idea advanced by the author and others, and now being operationalized in the proliferation of school-based clinics.

Multi-purpose youth serving agencies are another type of facility used by male adolescents. The Door, A Center for Alternatives, has been most often cited as the model that includes medical, recreational, creative, educational, vocational and other social interventions. In its early years, it gained its reputation as a place of intense caring for young people, a vast shelter created by committed idealists to enhance the lives of troubled young people. As the funding realities have begun to emerge and times have changed, the Door is considered more "establishment" than previously (e.g. the staff is paid competitive professional salaries). Nevertheless, it continues to serve thousands of New York City youngsters and has been replicated in several places including overseas (see section on International). Each month, more than 1,200 young people aged 12 to 20 take advantage of the many services provided, all free of charge.

Several years ago, the Door implemented a new program with the goal of providing sex education and birth control counseling to 700 adolescent males annually (Summary of Program Status, 1987). Because of its diverse and heavily utilized program, males could be recruited from other Door services through the efforts of a charismatic full-time male counselor. More than 500 young men received medical services as well as counseling on contraception, sexuality and AIDS in the Adolescent Health Center. A variety of weekly discussion groups and workshops were attended by almost 2,000 boys, in both co-educational and male only groupings, with components directed toward relationships, self-esteem, and decision making, using films, video and role-models.

A new policy requires that all Door members have a physical examination in the Adolescent Health Center to assess risk behaviors, particularly related to AIDS. Males also receive birth control information and education, a review of reproductive anatomy and contraception, AIDS risk information and safer sex practices (a similar protocol is provided to females). In addition to these scheduled programs, the Door has conducted what they call special "inreach" programs: a mobile contraceptive wagon in honor of Valentine's Day; classes in Spanish on contraception and reproductive physiology for young people attending ESL classes at the Door's Learning Center; a young fathers' program. Because the Door has a "captive audience" in a very large and attractive facility, spontaneous and innovative events can be easily implemented. Door staff make presentations in the community at schools and health fairs and network with hundreds of community agencies.

The Hub: Center for Change for South Bronx Teens is another version of the comprehensive youth-serving agency. Organized by Planned Parenthood of New York City in 1981, it has a special focus on pregnancy prevention and special interest in recruiting young males from the neighborhood. Medical and enrichment needs are met in one facility. One floor houses a family planning clinic; another floor contains facilities for educational programs that include extensive job-related counseling and vocational skills. The Hub's Computer Corps provides training in programming and word processing; graduates receive help in finding part-time jobs. A peer after school tutorial program in math and reading offers homework assistance. Sexuality education is covered in workshops on site or in the local schools.

Recreational programs such as dance, theater, karate and body-building are also available on site. One unique project provides young graffiti artists with instruction and space to practice their art. A social services counselor is responsible for making home and school visits to assist Hub clients. While the Hub program has not been evaluated, enrollment is high and the participants and staff appear to be enthusiastic about the approach.

One of the most interesting new programs to emerge out of this more holistic approach to pregnancy prevention is called Multi-Service Family Life and Sex Education Program. This program reflects the thinking and direction of Michael Carrera, who put together the various program components using collaborative partners from a number of agencies with the Children's Aid Society as the lead agency. There are seven Primary Prevention Programmatic Dimensions:

1. Medical and health services—available on site each week, complete physical annually, with contraceptive counseling and prescription. Enrollees receive complete health history profiles. Weekly follow-up counseling of contraceptive patients.

2. Self-esteem enhancement through the performing arts—weekly workshops with parents and teens led by professionals from National Black Theatre. Issues include conflict resolution, job problems, family roles, gender roles, etc. Use music, dance, role play and drama.

3. Lifetime individual sports—skills training in squash, tennis, golf and swimming; skills that emphasize self-discipline, self-control and a precise mastery.

4. Academic assessment and homework help program—each teen is given a complete educational needs assessment and prescription for individual and group tutorials, given by volunteers and educational experts. In addition, homework help is available two afternoons a week.

5. College admissions program—every participant receives a certificate at the beginning of the program guaranteeing a place as a Freshman at Hunter College following completion of the teen pregnancy prevention program and graduation from high school. All college costs will be subsidized.

6. Family life and sex education program—15 week, two hour weekly, separate programs for parents and teens, with a holistic view of sexuality, using readings, films, role playing and lectures. A graduation ceremony and dinner is held at completion of the unit. Parents and adults in the community are encouraged to participate. Child care is available for parent sessions.

7. Job club and career awareness program—a weekly two hour program conducted by employment specialists to help teens explore career possibilities, secure a social security card, complete working papers and apply for jobs. Each teen secures a job either at the site or off, or as part of an Entrepeneurial Apprenticeship Program. Each participant opens a bank account and contributes to it weekly.

Through the program, contact is made with each parent and each teen every day; every evening a session for them is scheduled. Although this is very labor intensive, it sends a clear message that the participants are valued and their participation is important. Carrera does much of the personal counseling and staff training and two hospitals provide contract medical personnel. There are specialists in employment, educational assessment, sexuality counseling and theater arts. Volunteers from the Junior League are used for mentoring.

Based on a preliminary evaluation, the potentiality for pregnancy prevention appears to be great. Since the program began, none of the boys have fathered a child. None of the participants have dropped out of school.

Adolescent health care units in hospital outpatient settings have been quite successful in recruiting males. These facilities are generally associated with medical schools that train physicians in the relatively new field of adolescent medicine. Robert Johnson reports that 70 percent of patients at the Adolescent Clinic of the University Hospital of the New Jersey College of Medicine in Newark are boys. These young men, aged 12 to 23, are most likely to first visit the clinic for treatment for infectious diseases (STDs or respiratory), followed by routine medical care such as physical examinations. However, increasing numbers are coming in for personal counseling. This is a very large service (over 5,000 visits a year); many of the patients come back repeatedly because they know they will find a sympathetic person. Johnson points out that with the ability to deliver comprehensive services, the staff can respond to the wide range of needs teenagers have. One of the clinic's goals is to teach these patients good health habits.

The Adolescent Clinic at the University of Washington offers primary medical services for teens and 24-hour emergency services. A number of school-based clinics have been organized and are operated by staff from hospital-based adolescent health services.

Health Maintenance Organizations (HMO) can also be utilized for male involvement programs. Ross Danielson has designed an intervention for the Oregon Kaiser Permanente Center, using trained nurse practitioners who present a slide tape and counseling on reproductive health to young male clinic visitors. In a control case study, he found participants had increased knowledge and expressed greater willingness to practice birth control (but found no significant behavioral changes). Community health centers could theoretically use these educational and counseling techniques to work with their young male patients.

School-based Clinics

*A*t least until the age of 16, schools are where young males most at risk can be found. There is growing literature on school-based clinics (Dryfoos and Klerman, 1988; Lovick, 1987; Kirby, 1985; U.S. Senate, 1985) and therefore the discussion here will focus on males and pregnancy prevention.

Currently there are at least 125 clinics operated by health or youth agencies in schools around the country. About 35 percent of clients of school-based clinics are males, but the range is wide, depending on the site. The DuSable Health Center in Chicago enrolled a very high proportion of the student body in its first year of operation (84 percent of females and 79 percent of males). Not all enrollees utilized the clinic. However, more males (55 percent) than females (53 percent) made visits during the year. Data from the Adolescent Health Care Program in Houston (one clinic that serves seven schools) show the reason for initial visits by males was most likely to be for athletic physicals (59 percent), followed by general health care and minor acute illnesses (30 percent). Less than one percent of the male patients made initial visits for family planning. Females presented for athletic physicals as well (36 percent); however, 30 percent of female's first visits were for family planning and only 19 percent for general care and minor illnesses. The Kansas City school clinics reported a sharp drop in non-use of contraceptives among males, from 45 percent in 1983 to 26 percent in 1985.

To a significant level, teen males appear to be interested in issues related to sexuality and contraception and in some school-based clinics, they receive the same care as teen females. Aaron Shirley, director of the school-based program in Jackson, Mississippi, in his testimony before the U.S. Senate Children's Public Police Forum, described,

> ...special counseling efforts coupled with specific health education session with...groups of 15-20, boys and girls mixed...These students are carried through a series of rap sessions which include discussions of possible adverse medical and economic consequences of pregnancies occurring during the teen years. During the course of each of the topics the responsibility of the male in pregnancy prevention is stressed...individual counseling sessions

result from the group activity wherein students who may be too shy to express themselves in a group...are able to sit with a counselor on an individual basis and work through various problems...

We have been pleasantly surprised at the type of open and trusting relationship which we have been able to establish with our students. This has allowed us, without any notion of invasion of privacy, to establish a monitoring and follow-up system of students (both boys and girls) who receive contraceptive devices and drugs...every student requesting family planning services is provided appropriate counseling which must be documented prior to receiving any contraceptive prescription or device...personal contact is made monthly with every recipient of contraceptives to enforce compliance as well as the various points covered in the health education sessions.

Our initial fears of possible resentment of this intrusion into the personal lives of our young participants were quickly relieved...to the contrary, our male students actually appreciated the attention they were receiving from us and the girls enjoyed the notion that someone truly cares about their well being.

This testimony summarizes a comprehensive approach to reaching young males: sex education with stress on personal responsibility, counseling, medical services, provision of contraception, follow-up and support. It is particularly impressive that all of this can be carried out under one roof, and that the roof is on the school house. However, there are as yet no hard data to substantiate that this approach will be more successful than others at prevention of unplanned pregnancies.

Several programs have been identified that reach young men in high schools by providing physical exams or making them available. The Teenage Health Clinic of the Baylor College of Medicine in Houston, Texas uses a clinic-on-wheels, parked on school campuses. According to Peggy Smith, the coaches from inner-city high schools have been the primary referral source for this service. An earlier version of this model placed the clinic in a YMCA, used health educators as counselors and worked a family planning message into the sports physical exam. The same health educators worked first in the schools, teaching a core prevention course and recruiting clinic patients. The students were given appointments at the clinic with encouragement from school coaches.

A school-based program, the Fifth Ward Enrichment Program, focuses on teaching sexual responsibility to 11-13 year old boys as part of the Urban Affairs Corporation school-based clinic program in Houston. Created and operated by Ernest McMillan, the program has all male staff who work with high risk youth using a system of positive reinforcement, intensive counseling, daily tutoring sessions, field trips, life skills workshops and academic guidance. The program includes the full services of the health center and functions all year round. Preliminary evaluation suggests that the participants are doing better in school and having fewer incidences of conduct disorder (McMillan, 1987). Staff reported increased recognition among boys that "they won't have children if they can't support them."

Schools are being used as places for recruitment to family planning clinics. In Baltimore,

65

a demonstration project was operated by Johns Hopkins University in two schools and the Self Center family planning clinic. A nurse practitioner and a social worker were placed in the schools where they conducted preliminary health screening and offered health education and counseling. Students were referred by them to the clinic for examinations and contraceptive prescriptions.

At the end of three years, the program was evaluated to determine the effect on pregnancy rates (Zabin et al., 1986). The two experimental schools were compared to two control schools. Among the female students in the program, pregnancy rates dropped 30 percent compared to a 58 percent increase in the non-participating schools. Male students in the program schools were much more likely to have attended a birth control clinic than non-program students, and much more likely to have used a method of birth control at last intercourse. Laurie Zabin remarks, "One of the most striking findings from the project is (that) the boys in the junior high school used the clinic as freely as girls of the same age. In view of the growing call for research into ways of attracting male clients to such facilities, the interest shown by these boys appears to be of some importance." The success of this project is attributed to the availability of high-quality, free services and intensive counseling by committed staff.

In Detroit, the local health department sponsors Teen Stop, a team of health workers who visit schools each week and set up appointments in neighborhood clinics for family planning visits. This service seemed to be utilized only by females, although in theory it would be appropriate for reaching males and offering them physical examinations that include sexuality counseling.

The Corner, a comprehensive health center for youth in Ypsilanti, Michigan, is operated in a school building used for vocational and adult education classes. While not officially linked to the school system, clinic personnel are welcomed into schools to present health and sex education classes. The clinic provides a wide range of services at low cost with a great deal of individual attention given to each young client. Males are encouraged to use the services but the vast majority of the clients are females. One of the most successful aspects of the program involves pregnant and parenting teenagers; attempts are made to involve teen fathers, although that is a difficult task.

The Corner is similar to a school-based clinic, but it is not located in a junior or senior high school nor does it receive any in-kind support from the school system. It operates all year long and can offer services to students and non-students during evenings and weekends. One of the criticisms of school-based clinics has been that in some areas with security problems, the buildings may shut down after school hours. Budgeting additional funds for security guards has been one solution to this problem. In Houston and Dallas, school-based clinics are located in out-buildings, creating greater access through longer hours and the capacity to accept clients who are not currently enrolled in school.

Youth-serving Agencies

*T*oday most organizations that serve young people have incorporated some form of family life education into their program content. The Girls Clubs of America and the YMCA have exemplary programs, as might be expected in agencies concerned with the role of females in today's society. A few of the agencies directed at boys have also developed programs. The Boys Clubs of America has a well-defined approach to the issue of pregnancy prevention, in contrast to the Boy Scouts, which has been slow to incorporate sexuality-related interventions into their scouting programs.

In the early 1970's, Boys Clubs initiated a program in family life and sexuality education with training modules developed by Michael Carrera at Hunter College. Learning activities on sexuality were also included in the Body Works program, an educational approach to comprehensive health promotion. There are 1,100 Boys Clubs around the nation serving 300,000 girls and a million boys who are mostly low-income urban children aged 6 to 18.

Recently Boys Clubs has initiated a new approach to the issue of male responsibility. Rather than focusing on decision making, it will concentrate on teaching members skills to: recognize and resist peer and social pressures, "say no" to drugs, alcohol and sex, and work with parents to deliver a consistent message to their children. The national office, after reviewing a number of approaches, selected three successful interventions they have piloted in ten demonstration sites: the Life Skills curriculum, developed by Gilbert Botvin and tested in smoking and alcohol abuse programs; Postponing Sexual Involvement developed by Marion Howard; and Project Smart, another drug abuse program, developed by the University of California.

The experience in the ten demonstration sites formed the basis of Boys Clubs' new national prevention program, Smart Moves. Program components are age-appropriate, involve parents, and provide inservice training for staff, volunteers, and prevention teams. Boys Club affiliates also conduct a wide array of educational, recreational and social programs including tutoring and after-school athletics. Roxanne Stillett, Program Director, points out that the Boys Clubs' clientele is not as tuned into pencil and paper activities as they are interested in more active pursuits, an important consideration in a non-school setting.

Programs That "Add On" Pregnancy Prevention

*I*ncreasingly, programs that have been organized for other purposes are adding components of family life education and birth control services to their roster of services. The Job Corps is an excellent example of this approach. Set up to provide vocational training and job placement, based in residential units, the Job Corps offers intensive skills training and counseling in a wide range of subjects. The Job Corps program in El Paso, Texas focuses on Hispanic male and female students residing in a refurbished motel; participants are presented with a very strong message that their job prospects would suffer if they were to have an unplanned child (Ridgely, 1985). This concept is reinforced through initial orientation sessions in family planning and health education, films, lectures, and discussions on sexuality topics with trained staff family planning counselors. An on-campus clinic provides free physical examinations and free contraceptives. Because of the Hispanic culture, the staff of this program feel it is particularly important to stress the male role in pregnancy prevention. As a result, more than half of the students seeking the advice of the counselors are males.

A large demonstration project operated by Public/Private Ventures in five pilot sites (junior highs) incorporates family life planning and birth control information into school enrichment and job training. STEP, the Summer Training Employment Program, has demonstrated greater use of contraception among young male participants.

In theory, any youth serving program can "add on" family life and sexuality education and condom distribution. One challenge for advocates of male involvement will be to raise the consciousness of youth workers and policy makers about the importance of these services. The connection has to be made between dropout prevention, employment training and pregnancy prevention. The initiation of national, state and local "Youth-at-Risk" coalitions, conferences and task forces provides an excellent opportunity for further program development.

AIDS Prevention Programs

*I*ronically, much of the new interest in reaching males emanates from concern about AIDS. Although the number of reported cases is still low among adolescent males, some are at high risk for AIDS because they are at high risk for intravenous drug use and sexually transmitted diseases. Concern has been expressed about the chain of heterosexual partners of members of high risk groups who may form a bridge to a much larger adolescent population in the near future. Currently, Black and Hispanic youth living in poverty areas have the highest prevalence rates. Geographically, cases of AIDS among teenagers are clustered in New Jersey, New York and Miami. However, the fear of AIDS is nationwide; recent surveys show a high proportion of teens expressing apprehension about the spread of the disease, but a much lower proportion altering their conduct. One survey found that while 85 percent of the teen respondents knew about risk factors, only five percent had changed their sexual behavior.

We have heard much more about condoms in the past year than ever before, with everyone including the President and the Pope offering an opinion about whether or not condoms should be mentioned in AIDS prevention programs. Surgeon General Koop has repeatedly called for sex education beginning in early grades and has advocated that courses instruct students on the use of condoms as a means of reducing the risk of transmitting the AIDS virus. The Centers for Disease Control has launched a major education initiative, including TV spots built around the theme "America Responds to AIDS." (However, major networks are still reluctant to accept condom advertising.) CDC has funded a number of national and state education organizations such as the National PTA and the National Organization of Black City Officials to work with schools and other agencies to convey AIDS prevention information at the community level. Funds for teacher training and materials development are also being provided to states and localities.

In the wake of rising concern about AIDS, states such as Rhode Island and Kansas, which previously were unwilling to mandate sex education, are now mandating AIDS education. At least 18 states have mandated AIDS education and many are in the process of developing curricula, training teachers and assisting local school systems. At the local level, parents have been heavily involved in curriculum review. As one educator put it, "AIDS is the most serious problem schools will face in the next 20 years." Some 41 states have adopted policies pertaining to persons with AIDS in school. In response to the unprecedented demand, AIDS curricula are being produced by many sources along with pamphlets, films, discussion guides and other materials.

Karen Hein, in a 1987 report to the Carnegie Foundation suggests a wide range of AIDS prevention activities, using many of the same approaches outlined in the previous sections: peer counselors, hot lines, networking between adolescent health facilities, curriculum development, and widespread condom distribution. Debra Haffner (1987) believes AIDS prevention programs should have four goals: to reduce panic and misinformation through education programs; to help teens postpone sexual initiation by teaching them resistance skills; to promote condom use; and to prevent drug use. Both Hein and Haffner emphasize the importance of involving teens in the design and implementation of AIDS prevention programs as peer leaders and in other roles.

Hein has operationalized her planning ideas in the design of a model Adolescent AIDS Program at the Montefiore Medical Center in New York. A multi-disciplinary team of physician, social worker, nurse practitioner and psychologist provide services and support to a very high risk population. They also conduct educational outreach and recruitment in the community and local schools.

Only through many years of great effort have condom distribution programs for pregnancy prevention gained acceptance. Efforts such as the Male Place and Three-for-Free described above are unique. The AIDS epidemic has spawned new condom distribution programs that appear to have had much shorter gestations. A recent report from the Aaron Medical Center (AMC) in the heart of Appalachia recounts the distribution of 3,000 "AIDS Prevention Kits," including educational materials and a Trojan condom in a fire engine red wrapper (HealthLink, 1987). "The real key to the success (no negative feedback) is that we delivered them to people's houses," explained Phil Aaron, Director of the Center. "We had runners—local kids...It was strictly person-to-person; that's what did it."

Many family planning clinics and adolescent health centers are struggling with the difficult ethical and organizational issues that arise in developing an AIDS program. HIV screening requires extensive counseling and/or referral to other community facilities for care.

VI
Organizational
Strategies

*T*here are a few organizations that have demonstrated an interest in the issue of male involvement. As one reviews the literature, the role of Planned Parenthood in male participation becomes clear. For almost two decades at the national level and through affiliates, PPFA has been trying to develop models for reaching and serving males. Most of the clinic based programs in the past were initiated through affiliates.

Recently, other national organizations have become interested in the issues surrounding male involvement in pregnancy prevention programs. The Center for Population Options, American Public Health Association, Children's Defense Fund, National Family Planning and Reproductive Health Association and National Urban League sponsored workshops and conferences, produced publications and conducted other activities in support of this concern. The problems surrounding teen fatherhood have also been discussed at conferences organized by state and national adolescent pregnancy coalitions. In addition, five states, New Jersey, Maine, North Carolina, Illinois and Indiana had statewide conferences specifically focused on male involvement. One state, Illinois, has an operating Male Adolescent Network (IMAN), supported by the Ounce of Prevention Fund.

Since 1987, a quarterly newsletter, *Men's Reproductive Health*, has been published by Douglas Beckstein, long an advocate of male service programs. This publication serves as a clearinghouse for program descriptions and policy issues. A survey of early subscribers showed the topics of greatest interest to be condoms, AIDS, teen fathers, minority men and school-based clinics. A directory of men's reproductive health programs is compiled and published by Beckstein annually. *Family Life Educator*, a quarterly Network publication, presents timely articles on a broad range of relevant subjects with research reviews and teaching tools.

The Center for Health Training in Seattle received a Title X grant to produce a bibliography on *Male Involvement in Family Planning*. Lynn Peterson, Project Consultant, has included 40 program descriptions and extensive listings of pamphlets, posters, curricula and films.

Planned Parenthood Federation of America

*T*he national Planned Parenthood organization has a long history of supporting male involvement. During the early 1960's, affiliates were being urged by national staff to develop more outreach to males; information about male involvement was passed along through regional workshops, national annual meetings and printed materials with particular emphasis on college students.

Today there are 183 local affiliates but (as mentioned above) few have developed successful on-going male involvement programs at the clinic level. About two out of five affiliates offer specific educational programs for men. Most affiliates have some forms of outreach such as peer programs, teen theater groups, hot lines, school presentations and/or other educational and motivational approaches for boys and girls in high school. In recent years, Planned Parenthood Federation of America has once again addressed the issue of male involvement and now views it as an important new mission. David Andrews, Executive Vice President, has spelled out five strategies for serving males:

1. Reaching males when they are young through educational in-school programs that involve parents with special focus on younger boys (10 to 12 year olds).
2. Developing the concept of primary health care where families go for services, moving away from the image of women's health care.
3. Promoting condom use. (Planned Parenthood produced and distributed its own brand of condoms for a short time but was priced out of the market by the cost of liability insurance.)
4. Developing public information campaigns. Using public service announcements telling males about the consequences of unwanted pregnancies.
5. Changing the composition of agency boards of directors by adding males with ideas about male services.

Andrews recognizes the difficulty that affiliates experience in obtaining funding for reaching male clients and convincing males, especially adolescents, to come to women's clinics for supplies. As an answer to this problem, Andrews proposes to develop a community-based distribution scheme. Teens would be trained as peer counselors and set up in business to sell condoms at low cost but with a small profit for the seller.

Susan Newcomer, Director of the Department of Education at PPFA, reports a high level of interest in male programs among affiliates, with heightened activity in response to the AIDS crisis. However, affiliates still find it difficult to recruit boys as clinic patients because of financial, psychological and programmatic constraints. An annotated bibliography, *Men and Sexuality*, has been produced by Newcomer's department.

American
Public Health
Association

*F*or a number of years, a Task Force on Men's Involvement in Family Planning and Reproductive Health has been sponsored by the Population section of APHA. This Task Force is operated by volunteers and its leaders have been strong advocates for male involvement programs around the country. The Task Force meets annually at national APHA meetings and beginning in 1987, at regional meetings in four sites. A mailing list of interested APHA members includes 600 names, giving evidence of the large and growing constituency for male programs. At the 1987 APHA Annual Meeting, the Task Force sponsored a double session that attracted an audience of 150. The session dealt with innovative materials and barriers to contraceptive programs for males.

According to Kevin McNally, co-chair of the Task Force (with Ann Plunkett), the Task Force's major concern is the removal of restrictions on the use of Title X funding for male clients. A major accomplishment was the approval by the APHA Governing Council of a policy resolution entitled "Collecting Data on Males Served by Federally Funded Family Planning Programs" (McNally, 1988). This resolution urges the federal government to count males served in clinics. This means changing the counting procedures on the Bureau's Common Reporting Requirements (BCRR) form to include males, and incorporating the number of males served in the funding allocation formula that currently only gives credit for serving low-income women. Governing Council approval means the entire APHA lobbying capacity can be directed toward this issue and gives the Task Force much greater credibility and strength.

In addition to organizing meetings and program sessions, the Task Force has stimulated the conducting of surveys of men's programs in different parts of the country (Swanson and Forrest, 1987; Levine, 1985). An occasional newsletter has been published by volunteers, with a boost from the APHA Population Section who awarded them a small grant for continuation. For several years, the Task Force organized continuing education sessions prior to the APHA meetings. The 1988 Task Force Goals include:
- Urge the Office of Family Planning to count men as clients on BCRR.
- Investigate FDA policy on quality control of condoms and urge FDA to publicize results of its recent research and testing.

- Develop a roster of experienced trainers in Men's Reproductive Health.
- Begin development of model protocols for male involvement and clinical services for men.
- Expand Task Force activities to involve more national organizations that impact men's health.

These goals provide a useful overview of current male involvement issues because the Task Force represents a cross-section of leaders and activists. It is interesting to note the heavy emphasis on condoms and training. Because their concerns extend to the broad issues of men's reproductive health and male sexuality, adolescents are not targeted.

Center for Population Options

*T*he Center for Population Options (CPO) is the only national agency whose entire focus is adolescent pregnancy. A number of CPO activities are directed toward informing young people, both boys and girls, about alternatives to parenthood and helping them make appropriate decisions. The following strategies have been promulgated by CPO:

- Giving technical assistance and training to national youth organizations in program development for sexuality and family planning education, including Big Brothers, Boys Clubs, 4-H Clubs, YMCA and church organizations.
- Implementing the *Life Planning* curriculum, a learning package that combines identifying educational and vocational directions with decision making about sexuality and family planning.
- Promoting sexual responsibility in the media through public service announcements, technical assistance to improve the quality of programming and working closely with the entertainment community to raise consciousness about population and family planning issues.
- Developing a Support Center for School-based Clinics that provides technical assistance to emerging programs, publishes *Clinic News* (a quarterly newsletter), organizes conferences and serves as coordinator of this emerging field.
- Developing materials regarding AIDS prevention programs and organizing national conferences.
- Holding a national conference on male involvement programs and issuing a report on the proceedings.

National Urban League

*T*he National Urban League has become heavily involved in the teenage pregnancy issues in recent years (Dryfoos, 1985). In addition to working with its 113 affiliates to stimulate family life education programs and support services for young parents, a national media campaign directed toward males has been launched. The campaign has produced a 60-second radio spot and posters that promote thinking before action. The radio spot features name entertainers singing a catchy tune that speaks to the "macho" young male. The poster slogans include "Not all brothers should be fathers," and "Don't make a baby if you can't be a father."

The campaign was designed and produced by a Black advertising firm and has been endorsed by major Black communication and media organizations. The posters were made by prisoners in the Greenhaven Prison. These materials have been made available to Urban League affiliates. The radio spot tag and the poster tell people to call or stop by the local Urban League office for further information.

Another strategy the Urban League hopes to pursue is the involvement of community organizations at the local level to help the Urban League enhance male participation in pregnancy prevention. Such groups as the Elks, men's clubs, lodges and fraternities are viewed as excellent sources for developing interactive relationships between men and boys.

The Urban League media campaign is the first national initiative directed toward young Black males. As the president of the organization, John Jacob, has stated, "...we have to speak frankly to our young Black males and tell them that being a teenage father does not make you a man, and a smart thing to do is to avoid fatherhood at an early age."

Edward Pitt, Director of Health Services, has a high level of commitment to the issue of unintended pregnancy. He has stressed the need for working at the community level. However, he feels there is a great lack of program expertise, particularly in regard to reaching males. He would like to see program models, in the form of how-to manuals, that could be readily implemented by community groups for such components as outreach, recruitment, clinic services, condom distribution and follow-up. One such publication, *Adolescent Male Responsibility: A Program Development Guide*, has recently been produced by the NUL staff (National Urban League, 1987). Forty programs that serve young males are annotated; 10 of these projects are operated by local Urban League affiliates.

The Ounce of Prevention Fund

*T*he Ounce of Prevention Fund is a statewide public/private umbrella organization, supported by the Illinois Department of Children and Family Services and the Harris Foundation. An examination of the activities performed by its 125 constituent Parents Too Soon agencies convinced program administrator Linda Miller that there was a shortage of male-oriented programs. IMAN, the Illinois Male Adolescent Network, was organized by Ounce member Curt Davies to encourage agencies to start programs, support the 13 agency programs that existed, and develop a model male involvement program curriculum. Examples of new starts include: the Mental Health Services of Southern Madison County which will train coaches to work with boys on decision making; Madison County Urban League which will conduct workshops for 10-15-year-old boys from female-headed households; and Planned Parenthood of Mid-Central Illinois which will involve young males in their Teens Care Too advisory council.

International
Programs

*T*he International Planned Parenthood Federation (IPPF) has assumed a major role in stimulating interest in the male involvement issue. In 1983, the IPPF organized a consultation of experts from around the world who produced an IPPF Strategy for Action and several publications. What is most interesting about the model and the summary report (IPPF, 1984) is its total applicability to the U.S. situation. While some of the language may differ ("change agents" for "outreach workers"), the concepts are the same:

- Men's ignorance about and/or opposition/indifference to family planning is a major constraint to program development.
- Joint decision making and shared responsibility should be the goal of all programs.
- Men have a right to family planning education and services.
- Rather than lecturing, program approaches should build on men's positive attitudes toward the value of children and family responsibilities.
- Program objectives include increasing the level of *knowledge*, encouraging male *support* for women's practice of family planning, and promoting *acceptance* and *practice* by men themselves.

The program guidelines summarized in the consultation report proposes:

> ...a strategy for men...developed as part of overall family planning programs. Preference should be given to integrating male components into on-going activities and to modifying or expanding...programs to meet men's needs...care should be taken to avoid isolating male family planning components and 'compartmentalizing' programs.

The Strategy for Action places heavy emphasis on training family planning workers to accommodate men by creating favorable clinic environments. The recommendations for international agencies are no different from the ideas presented below in the recommendations for U.S. adolescents. This suggests the universality of family planning programs targeted at low-income populations around the world. While we know that culture is an important determinant of fertility behavior, these program approaches suggest that males in many different settings have similar needs, and that "men's very real involvement in

81

decisions about contraception and family planning is seldom formally recognized...most programs are overwhelmingly designed for women" (IPPF, 1984).

The IPPF consultation helps us recognize that the U.S. family planning effort could probably be enhanced by learning from experiences in other countries. The recent AGI study of developed countries corroborates that point. Although my research did not encompass international programs, several models emerged that merit attention.

In Guatemala City, a teenage multipurpose center, "El Camino," offers sex education and contraceptive services (Andrade, 1984) along with recreation, vocational courses, tutoring programs, counseling, medical and dental assistance. A unique aspect of the program is the training and utilization of "youth multipliers" who recruit family planning patients through home visits and distribute condoms. In Mexico City, the Center for Adolescent Orientation (CORA), also a comprehensive program, serves more than 40,000 young people each year. The program uses peer teams to deliver contraceptives to youth in factories. These two efforts are similar to the New York based "Door."

Overseas programs appear to demonstrate much more flexibility about distribution of male contraceptives. In Japan, condoms are sold door-to-door and marketed with sophisticated packaging designed by commercial artists. Packages contain a cleaning towelette, reorder cards and instructions for products with names such as Yearn, Dream Special, Paradise and Lady Wet. In Thailand and South Korea, pills are distributed door-to-door along with condoms. However, home distribution reaches housewives and is probably not an effective means for reaching unmarried teenagers. The concept of social marketing, developed in these countries, places contraceptive sales at subsidized prices in established commercial channels using promotion and advertising to stimulate business. In Hong Kong, "Mr. Family Planning" is the symbol used to promote condom sales through vending machines in public toilets.

These are just a few programs compiled from the literature. Experience in other countries with community-based distribution and other forms of marketing is extensive. Very little of this type of activity has been undertaken in the U.S. because of the strong medical clinic model that has dominated the family planning field since Margaret Sanger opened her first Brownsville clinic in 1916.

VII
Financial
Support for
Programs

*T*he only major government source for funding of male involvement programs is the Office of Family Planning currently located in the Office of Population Affairs. This agency allocates family planning funds (Title X) through ten regional offices that administer family planning grants to the local level. Most of these grants are now consolidated at the state level and are distributed to delegate agencies through state health departments, state non-profit family coordinating agencies or statewide Planned Parenthood affiliates.

Prior to 1980, the federal family planning program was operated by the Bureau of Community Health Services (BCHS). In 1978, male involvement was singled out as an issue that required a special initiative. In that year, seventeen new male demonstration projects were funded for the purpose of improving male involvement in family planning decisions and contraceptive use. The 1979 plan from the BCHS called for a five-year expansion in services to males with a goal of reaching (presumably through educational services) some 200,000 males and providing clinical services to 60,000 males by 1983. In 1979, $600,000 was budgeted for this initiative, a figure that grew to one million dollars by 1981 and remained at that level until 1983. At the end of the five year period, services for females were projected to build to a level of funding over half-a-billion dollars, so the funding request for males would have been less than .002 percent of the budget. By 1980, the special initiative had disappeared from the planning process and presumably the seventeen programs were not refunded. Due to the change in administration, the Title X agency was moved out of the BCHS (which was dismantled) and the male initiative apparently discontinued. The current staff at DHHS cannot locate any reports from the initiative and whatever experience might have been gained at that time is lost to posterity.

In 1984, the Office of Family Planning launched a new initiative regarding male involvement. A half million dollars (Title X) was given to each region for special programs: natural family planning, family involvement, infertility services and/or male involvement. Grantees were invited to submit proposals and regional officers then selected 20 male involvement programs from around the country. The regional allocations, therefore, were split in a number of ways so the grants were quite small for each effort. A number of grantees have been interviewed and the findings are incorporated where appropriate. There are no reporting requirements except numbers of users and encounters. It is unlikely that any new documentation will emerge from this venture.

A major barrier to development of Title X services for males was created in 1982 when the Office of Family Planning stopped counting male clients. Clinics were discouraged from using scarce funds for males because allocation formulae are based on females served.

Over the years, small amounts of Title X money have been granted to the Job Corps, including funds for educating males in special twelve week training sessions. Theoretically, Title X funds that pass through the National Institutes for Health could be used for research and demonstration projects. Only one research grant, on the biological social factors in adolescent fertility (Udry, 1985) has been used as a resource for this study.

A few demonstration projects directed toward males have been funded through the Office of Adolescent Pregnancy Programs, using Title XX, Adolescent Family Life Act (AFLA) funds. The Urban League initiated several male responsibility affiliates with AFLA support. The Kaiser HMO nurse-practitioner research was also supported by AFLA.

Several model male programs are currently being funded by state and local health agencies, for example, Male's Place with county health department funds in North Carolina and Three-For-Free by the Maryland State Department of Health. Medicaid funds could in theory be used to reimburse clinics and private physicians for services to young males who are Medicaid eligible. Under the EPSDT program, states are required to provide periodic screening, diagnosis and treatment to all medically needy children under age 21. These funds are currently being used in some health clinics and school-based programs for physical examinations that include family planning. In California, Medicaid reimburses for condoms only if prescribed by a physician. In a few states, Social Services Title XX funds are being used to subsidize clinic services to male patients.

Foundations have been more likely to support adolescent father programs than programs directed toward involving males in pregnancy prevention. No large scale research or demonstration project specifically focused on adolescent males has been funded by a foundation. However, foundations have been instrumental in supporting school-based clinics, evaluation of the impact of programs, and media campaigns with materials targeted to males.

Funds for sex education and family planning services of all kinds are scarce in the 1980s. Many educational and motivational initiatives are directed at both boys and girls, so at least for those types of initiatives, programs can expect support, even if limited. However, prospects for specific categorical funding of male involvement programs by either the public or the private sector appear to be low, just as they have been in the past.

The action of the American Public Health Association at the 1987 Annual Meeting, adopting a resolution that supports the resumption of counting males in Title X funded clinics, may signal the beginning of changing attitudes on the importance of this issue. At the same time, the AIDS crisis is generating new funds that can be used for screening, testing and counseling. We do not know what the implications are of mixing services and funding of pregnancy prevention and AIDS detection.

VIII
Recommendations

This review of programs and services directed toward young males serves as a background for proposing a series of objectives that might be met by various interventions with an overall goal of fostering responsible sexual behavior on the part of adolescent boys:

- To help boys understand the need for a *shared responsibility* for pregnancy prevention.
- To give boys *knowledge* of the basics of reproduction, sexuality, contraception and pregnancy.
- To give boys *access* to condoms.
- To advertise the *message* of sexual responsibility.
- To change the *environment* in family planning clinics to make them more acceptable to males.
- To add family planning for males to *comprehensive health care services*, particularly at school-based clinics.
- To teach boys to *communicate* with girls (and vice versa).
- To broaden *life options* for all young people.

These objectives provide the framework for a discussion of implementation strategies. It should be noted that interventions to delay intercourse are not included here. There is no evidence that this approach by itself would have any effect on boys; we do not even know whether it has an effect on girls. It is possible boys can be convinced to delay initiation of intercourse, but it is difficult to imagine that this behavioral change would result from training in "saying no" skills. The decision to delay would more likely be influenced by a deeper understanding of the long-term consequences of early unprotected intercourse on both the partner and the boy himself. Granted, this is a large assignment in a society where many young boys are sexually active long before they reach the cognitive level needed to appreciate the implications.

In a culture where premarital sex has become a norm, it is more realistic to develop strategies aimed at prevention and protection. If every boy initiated sex fully protected (using a condom), pregnancy rates, STD rates and AIDS rates would fall.

Eight objectives have been proposed here based on the common sense rule. It stands to reason that if strategies for implementing objectives were pursued, boys might grow up to be more competent and sensitive. However, these recommendations are really a package, no single strategy will be effective without most of the others. Just as girls need the capacity and the motivation to avoid early maternity, boys must gain knowledge, be given the equipment and have a sense of the future if they are to exercise the amount of internal control society expects from them.

This view, that not one intervention will have much of an impact unless it is part of a package that begins to alter the social environment, is supported by the findings of the recent AGI study of policies regarding teenage pregnancy in other Western developed countries. According to an editorial in *Family Planning Perspectives*, "What appears to be lacking in the U.S. is the political will exercised in the other countries to take necessary action." They cite as an example how Sweden's legalization of abortion was linked to improved sex education and the provision of contraceptive services for teenagers through schools and the health care system. In each of the other countries, AGI found a "clear-cut will to reduce levels of teenage pregnancy" on the part of the government, with focus on preventing pregnancy rather than preventing sexual activity (Jones, 1985).

Strategies for Implementing Objectives

*T*o Help Boys Understand the Need for Shared Responsibility

The idea that it takes two to make a baby should be presented to children at very early ages (and usually is). Obviously, the concept that a man has an equal responsibility with a woman for his children ought to be imbued through the family. Unfortunately, increasing numbers of children are being reared in households where father is nonexistent and mother is not available. This is one of those difficult areas where schools are being forced to take over for families in what could be perceived as the "moral development" of the child. Expecting schools to act as surrogate parents and to teach boys how to care for and respect girls may be unrealistic.

For schools with interest in the students' social development, a number of approaches can be used. Sex and family life education classes should include a discussion of family roles and a review of the consequences of early parenthood for the mother, father and baby. Many materials have been produced in this field, but only recently have they begun to be tailored to the boys' needs. Information about child support laws might be a useful addition for curricula directed toward junior and senior high school students.

A number of male outreach programs in clinics and youth serving agencies use innovative techniques to convince boys that they should have more consideration for their partners. One program tries to teach boys to be more sensitive by putting them through a simulated physical examination including a pelvic. The boys are told in great detail what girls have to experience in order to obtain contraception and what happens to girls who don't use contraception. Films are shown on the birth of a baby. Involving male partners in pregnancy counseling and abortion counseling is another approach to demonstrating to boys the importance of their roles. This is particularly important in minority communities where boys have very negative attitudes toward abortion.

Teaching young men to share responsibility with young women is an objective that transcends sexual relationships. It is a crucial value in all relationships and cannot be taught with one-shot inoculations of information or group processes. Role models, mentoring, and one-on-one interventions between responsible adults and young people may be useful for raising consciousness about the importance of caring. This is a major challenge in commu-

91

nities where young people increasingly are surrounded by evidence of non-caring.

In this sense, teaching responsibility is similar to raising self-esteem. A heightened sense of self-value arises from a more positive perception of how the society values one. It is difficult for a youngster to raise his or her own self-esteem in an adverse environment replete with negative messages and experiences. Thus, changes should be initiated by social institutions to help young boys become more productive members of society and change their perceptions about how they fit in.

*T*o Give Boys Knowledge

Boys are currently being offered sex education in schools but it is clear that the information they are receiving has no *salience* for them. Instruction must be age appropriate and tailored to developmental stages; attention must be paid to language and culture. Individual counseling would be useful for this effort.

The knowledge required by boys to become partners in the sexual relationship may also be acquired outside of schools. Recreational organizations, sports agencies and boys clubs are excellent loci for educational interventions. Films can be used to overcome language barriers and/or capture the imagination and interest of the target audience.

For boys who are sexually active, there are specific details that would help them become more involved in the process of pregnancy prevention. For example, they could be taught to keep track of their partner's menstrual cycle and told they could learn to participate in the insertion of the diaphragm. Some programs teach about "outercourse," sexual practices that do not include coitus.

Young men are very receptive to educational interventions that deal with sexuality. They are quite aware of their own ignorance and eager to learn the correct facts.

*T*o Give Boys Access to Condoms

Condoms are a crucial component of responsible male sexual behavior. Considerable evidence shows that condom distribution programs can effect both pregnancy rates and STD rates (at least in developing countries) and it seems reasonable to assume that if all boys used condoms, there would be an improvement in outcomes. Clearly, the AIDS epidemic adds urgency to this strategy. Condom use may save lives as well as prevent unwanted pregnancies.

The first line of strategy would be to actively promote use of condoms. Since the advent of family planning clinics and the placement of responsibility for birth control in the hands of women, condoms have received a "bum rap." They have suffered from poor reputation both in terms of efficacy and aesthetics. Yet failure rates are relatively low and many adherents claim that sensation can be enhanced through the use of modern condoms. Boys need to be convinced that condoms are where it's at. They have to be socialized to believe that with-it people use condoms.

Once the condom message is broadcast, the next problem is to make sure condoms are available. Distribution can be accomplished through multiple loci, such as recreational centers, gyms, factories and other work places, gas stations, pool halls, street corners, sports events, and even schools. Many more vending machines should be installed.

The barriers to condom distribution appear to be more attitudinal than functional. Family planning clinics have placed higher priority on medical methods and services for women. Although they have encouraged men to use the clinic services, the funding sources to which they are accountable often do not reimburse them for services to males.

Some young men are kept from purchasing condoms in drug and grocery stores because of embarrassment. Others do not have the cash when they need the contraceptives.

The most successful condom distribution systems give away condoms along with instructional materials in non-medical settings, wherever young men congregate. The methods seem to be more acceptable when distributed by older males (authority figures) from the same cultural background or community as the recipient.

It has been proposed that packaging of condoms be improved so all boys could carry them around in places other than wallets (where unused condoms may become defective over time). An attractive key chain attachment could be devised that would insure cleanliness and preservation (and certainly add to the boy's status in some groups). Clear instructions for use should be incorporated in the packaging. It has also been proposed that males be encouraged to carry around other non-prescription methods such as sponges, foam and jelly, as part of their commitment to shared responsibility.

*T*o Advertise the Message of Sexual Responsibility

This society has to come to a consensus that teenage pregnancy can be prevented. Every boy and girl has to grow up with the knowledge that each is in control of his or her sexual life and can make decisions about when to become parents. This is not just a problem of male involvement; it is a problem that involves all aspects of family, community and society. Giving messages to boys about responsibility is important, but none of this will have an effect unless it is part of a larger package of interventions that reaches into the lives of all young people.

Within the context of a general community effort to prevent teenage pregnancy, it is possible to develop some specific messages addressed to boys, especially since almost all of the prevention messages to date have been addressed to girls. There are already a number of media campaigns being developed that suggest to boys that they are partners in the act; in some, pregnancy prevention messages are tied in with employment information. The placement of messages can be on billboards, car cards, advertisements, through popular music, and in high school journals. Rock stars, sports figures and other "heroes" are used to deliver the message.

The most effective messages go beyond moral persuasion and make explicit where boys can go for help; they tell them where they can get counseling, VD information, condoms and other sex-related assistance. Programs set up information tables at health fairs and other places where young people congregate. They provide pamphlets and offer referrals to health, social and welfare agencies. Teen theater groups offer information in innovative ways.

Condom advertising and other sexually-related materials on TV and radio can have a major impact on increasing awareness about sexual responsibility. In this media-oriented society, it would give the message credibility and acceptability.

*T*o Change the Environment in Family Planning Clinics

Because of the funding restrictions and other problems referred to above, clinics may not be the appropriate place to reach large numbers of young males. For those clinics interested in recruiting male patients, it has been recommended that they make changes in the clinic environment so that males will feel more comfortable. Male staff appear to be an important component of male involvement programs; apparently in most clinics young males feel much more comfortable being counseled by same sex advisors. It has also been suggested that female staff members need special inservice training if they are going to deal with male clients. The clinic ambiance should be reviewed to make sure there are male oriented posters, pamphlets and reading materials.

Clinics should enhance male participation in pregnancy prevention by instructing females about how to involve males. Staff should encourage clients to bring in partners and invite them to join in the counseling and witness the physical examination. Contraceptive continuation is a critical component of prevention; male partners could be drawn into the follow-up process. One program is experimenting with contract counseling for pill patients; the male partner could become a party to the contract along with the female.

It should be acknowledged that any new components added to clinic protocol require staff time, and that means funds. At present, there are no funds for involving males in this process.

Abortion clinics should also involve males in the process. In some places, partners are encouraged to participate in the pregnancy counseling and decision making prior to the procedure. This should be standard practice. Males should also be urged to think about post-abortion contraception and given the joint responsibility for determining what method the couple will use in the future.

*T*o Add Family Planning for Males to Comprehensive Health Services

The experience being generated from school-based health clinics, comprehensive youth centers and hospital-based adolescent health programs suggests that young boys and girls feel more comfortable receiving their family planning instruction and equipment in the context of multi-service settings. This avoids the embarrassment of admitting to peers and parents that one is sexually active (although for boys, confidentiality may not be such an issue). For girls, school-based clinics can follow up on pill compliance. This aspect of the service is considered critical. Again, for boys, the subject is treated differently and up until the recent testimony by Aaron Shirley cited above, there has been little evidence either that boys who are sexually active and receive condoms are followed up, or that lowered pregnancy rates can be attributed to the male role.

It is a safe assumption that school-based clinics which combine sex education in classrooms, sexuality counseling in the clinic and *distribution of contraceptives* could have an important impact on boys. At the junior high school level, it is possible to work with younger boys, prior to their initiation of sexual activity, and combine social support systems with the provision of sexuality education. In these programs, mentors can be used to assist needy youngsters with a wide range of problems including homework, parent relationships and learning how to deal with peers—girls and boys.

Aside from school-based clinics, there are few places young men can go to get routine health care such as physical exams and treatment for minor problems such as acne and headaches. Many youngsters receive health care from their family physician and/or pediatrician where they go for annual physicals and acute care. Boys rarely talk to their family doctors about their developmental or sexual problems and most doctors are loathe to initiate discussion of these topics. Other youngsters, who do not have access to private medical care, receive all their services in hospital emergency rooms. The rationale for opening some of the school-based clinics has been the overload in emergency rooms produced by adolescent patients. While emergency rooms have the capacity for treating injuries and illnesses, they have no capability for counseling teenagers about sexual issues nor for providing them with contraception.

Community health centers and health maintenance organizations are organized to provide family medicine because they treat the whole family. Teenagers are often unwilling to use the facilities for sexually related services. The CHCs and the HMOs are not often organized to provide adolescents with the kinds of services they require: confidential, no hassle, convenient. However, there are exceptional programs (Kaiser Permanente) and it is possible that clinics could modify their services to accommodate the needs of adolescents.

Health services for males could be organized at the work place. Some industries employ nurses and some unions have health centers. Where health services are available, it would be possible to add on components of care that address sexuality, contraception and pregnancy prevention.

*T*o Teach Boys to Communicate with Girls (and Vice Versa)

Many boys are afraid to talk to girls about sex and contraception. This is not surprising since mothers and fathers have great difficulty talking to each other about the subject and find it nearly impossible to talk to their children. Few males are socialized to discuss these matters with their partners. While boys talk about sex with each other they are full of misinformation and worried that girls will find out how little they know.

Basic skills in communication might be easier to teach than some of the more abstract concepts such as "delayed gratification" and "shared responsibility" implicit in pregnancy prevention. Boys could be taught in any of the settings referred to above to always discuss with their partners means of protection against pregnancy *before* entering into a sexual encounter. They could be taught to offer to help pay for contraception if this is a problem for the partner (and even if it isn't).

Again, the objective of better communication between people should not be limited to the area of sexuality. Boys and girls and men and women (and agencies and nations) need to learn how to say what is on their minds, to show that they care for each other and to share a myriad of other feelings that must be conveyed between people if they are to have a satisfying relationship.

Girls in this society are socialized to talk about their feelings. Just as it is considered acceptable for a girl to cry, girls have more room in which to express their emotions. Nevertheless, they appear to lack the necessary skills to "say no" or to say "wait" even when that is what they want to do. This situation speaks to the need for working with both sexes together, helping them to talk to each other. However, a number of programs report that youngsters feel more comfortable in single sex discussion groups, at least at the junior high school level. Probably a combination of approaches would be most successful in opening up sensitive areas for discussion.

The locus for communication training could be any agency that has the capacity to serve youngsters. Some family life curricula include units on communication skills, and these courses are being taught in junior and senior high schools. The same curricula are adaptable to use in youth serving organizations, church groups, recreational centers and other places where young people congregate. Again, the principle of opening up communication should be incorporated in all of the interventions, in clinic services, outreach programs, condom distribution, consciousness-raising and other approaches.

To Broaden Life Options for All Young People

In the beginning of this book, an informant was quoted as saying that the most important strategy for pregnancy prevention among males was the provision of jobs. A clear picture emerges out of all of this verbiage showing that boys who become teen fathers suffer from many of the same disadvantages as girls who become teen mothers—low basic skills, alienation from school, growing up in single-head households, low socio-economic status compounded by minority status. The primary difference is that males can escape some of the consequences of early paternity by denying their role and refusing to contribute to the welfare of the child while the mother is invariably stuck with the responsibility.

So the lack of opportunity is a double-edged sword. Faced with the hopelessness and anomie of poverty, young boys engage in sex with little thought or concern about the aftermath and when the baby arrives, are faced with the same conditions, even if they want to support their child. Availability of jobs is clearly a key ingredient for prevention as well as amelioration of the adverse effects of pregnancy.

It is not the purpose of this report to dwell on the life options hypothesis. The array of services needed are large and urgent: school remediation, counseling, vocational guidance, skills training and job placement. There is increasing evidence that disadvantaged young boys and girls must have the support of a responsible adult to act as an advocate, mentor, role model and authoritative friend. They need someone to act as surrogate parent, in the absence of mothers and fathers who formerly provided support.

This is not really a question of male involvement. The word "involvement" implies that there is something going on that males should be brought *in* to. In this society, what they should be brought *in* to is the middle class and the situation is no different for deprived males than it is for deprived females. What "life options" implies is society's involvement with youth, insuring that all children have access to the quality of life that middle class adults now enjoy. That is the American Dream. It is unlikely that the incidence of teenage pregnancy will lessen very much until more gates are opened for disadvantaged youth.

IX
Priorities
for Action

*T*he life options approach is recommended as a framework for involving males; this means conceptualizing large-scale long-term institutional interventions that upgrade the quality of schools, increase job opportunities and provide support services. Community and statewide consortia may be the best instruments for these kinds of endeavors. Hopefully, a new administration in Washington will shift national priorities to the critical needs of youth.

Several short-term interventions are also important, can be implemented more readily, and are much less costly:

- Condom distribution must be implemented on a large scale through a variety of innovative approaches.
- More effective male service components must be developed and then implemented into existing family planning clinics. This implies extensive staff training.
- Expansion of school-based clinics and other comprehensive health, social-services, and recreational programs should be encouraged. Sexuality counseling and contraceptive distribution for males must be built into these holistic approaches.
- Promotion of the male role in decision making can be accomplished through media campaigns, role-models, peer programs and other creative efforts at consciousness raising.
- Connection between life options and pregnancy prevention should be made explicit in life planning and social skills training programs. Educational enrichment and employment efforts should include information on sexuality issues. Family planning programs should pay attention to broader social issues such as dropout and unemployment.

Additional data-gathering and research would enhance the state-of-the-art about male programs. The information base is still too limited to draw firm conclusions about new directions. The school-clinic project in Baltimore (Zabin, 1986) has produced excellent program evaluation data but the model has not been replicated elsewhere. The major national longitudinal surveys of youth (High School and Beyond and National Longitudinal Survey of Youth) are currently being mined to examine some of the issues explored in this book (determinants of sexual activity, contraceptive use, early paternity).

101

Finally, little evidence has been generated by this overview that argues for any special priority for programs for males except for condom distribution. And in theory, young females could benefit equally from greater access to condoms and foam. Rather, the research has verified the urgency for responding to the needs of disadvantaged youngsters, both boys and girls, generally in programs that are addressed to both. As has been stated repeatedly, there is little program evaluation to guide decision-makers. However, the needs are such that the decisions cannot await long-term evaluations. Program development and evaluation research can be initiated simultaneously, using the common sense rule to weight the distribution of funding support. Not every program needs to be a demonstration project.

References

Andrade, S.J. *Sex Education & Family Planning Services for Adolescents in Latin America: The Example of El Camino in Guatemala.* The Pathfinder Fund, Working Papers, No. 2, February 1985.

Andrews, D. "Shared Sexual Responsibility: A Strategy for Male Involvement." Paper presented at the American Public Health Association Annual Meeting, Anaheim, CA, 1984.

Armstrong, B. Personal communication with author, February 1988.

Arnold, C.B. "A Condom Distribution Program for Adolescent Males." In *Readings in Family Planning: A Challenge to the Health Professions*, pp. 138-145. Compiled by D.V. McCallister, V. Thiessen and H. McDermott. St. Louis, MO: C.V. Mosby Co., 1973.

Barro, S., and Kolstad, L. *Who Drops Out of High School?: Findings from High School and Beyond.* Washington, DC: Center for Education Statistics, U.S. Department of Education, 1987.

Berlin, G., and Sum, A. *Toward a More Perfect Union: Basic Skills, Poor Families and Our Economic Future.* Ford Foundation, 1988.

Blyth, B.J.; Gilchrist, L.; and Schinke, S. "Pregnancy Prevention Groups for Adolescents." *Social Work* 26(June 1981): 503-4.

Botvin, G. "Substance Abuse Prevention Efforts: Recent Developments and Future Directions." *Journal of School Health* 56:9(1986): 369-374.

Calderwood, D. "Male Sexual Health." *SIECUS Report* 13:2(1984): 1- 5.

Center for Population Options (CPO). "Local Success Story." *Issues and Action Update* 4:1 (1985): 3.

Center for Population Options (CPO). "Involving Parents in Sexuality Education Programs: The Role of Agencies Serving Youth." Washington, DC: Center for Population Options, 1984.

Chilman, C. *Adolescent Sexuality in a Changing American Society.* New York: John Wiley and Sons, 1983.

Chilman, C. Personal communication with author, 1985.

Clark, S.D. Personal communication with author, February 1988.

Clark, S.D.; Zabin, L.S.; and Hardy, J.B. "Sex, Contraception, and Parenthood: Experience and Attitudes Among Urban Black Young Men." *Family Planning Perspectives* 16:2(1984): 77-82.

Darabi, K. "Beyond Access: Preventing Early Pregnancy." Final report to the W.T. Grant Foundation, Center for Population and Family Health, Columbia University, 1984.

Davis, S.N., and Harris, M.B. "Sexual Knowledge, Sexual Interests and Sources of Sexual Information." *Adolescence* 17(Summer 1982): 471-92.

105

Department of Public Health, City of Toronto. "Male Sexuality Survey: Knowledge and Attitudes of Toronto Adolescents." Toronto, Canada: Family Planning Services, February, 1982.

Dryfoos, J. "School-based Clinics: A New Approach to Preventing Adolescent Pregnancy?" *Family Planning Perspectives* 17:2(1985): 70-75.

Dryfoos, J., and Klerman, L. "School-based Clinics: Their Role in Helping Students Meet the 1990 Objectives." *Health Education Quarterly* (Spring 1988).

Dryfoos, J. "Youth-at-Risk: One in Four in Jeopardy." Report to Carnegie Corporation, 1987.

Finkel, M.L., and Finkel, D.J. "Male Adolescent Contraceptive Utilization." *Adolescence* 13(1978): 443.

Finkel, M.L., and Finkel, D.J. "Sexual and Contraceptive Knowledge, Attitudes and Behavior of Male Adolescents." *Family Planning Perspectives* 7(1975): 256.

Gordon, P.H., and DeMarco, L. "Reproductive Health Services for Men: Is There a Need?" *Family Planning Perspectives* 16:1(1984): 44-46.

Gordon, S.; Scales, P.; and Everly, K. *The Sexual Adolescent: Communicating with Teenagers About Sex.* 2nd ed. N. Scituate, MA: Duxbury Press, 1979.

Graham, S. Personal communication with author, 1988.

Haffner, D. *AIDS and Adolescents.* Washington, DC: Center for Population Options, 1987.

Harris, L. and Associates. *American Teens Speak: Sex, Myths, TV, and Birth Control.* New York, 1986.

Hayes, C. (ed.). *Risking the Future.* Vol. 1. Washington, DC: National Academy of Sciences Press, 1987.

Healthlink (Special Issue on AIDS Education). December, 1987.

Hein, K. "AIDS in Adolescence: A Rationale for Action." Report to Carnegie Corporation, 1987.

Hogan, D.; Astone, N.; and Kitigawa, E. "Social and Environmental Factors Influencing Contraceptive Use Among Black Adolescents." *Family Planning Perspectives* 17:4(1985): 165-169.

International Planned Parenthood Federation (IPPF). *Male Involvement in Family Planning.* London: 1984.

Jones, E.; Forrest, J.D.; Goldman, N.; Henshaw, S.; Lincoln, R.; Westoff, C.F.; Rosoff, J.I.; and Wulf, D. "Teenage Pregnancy in Developed Countries: Determinants and Policy Implications." *Family Planning Perspectives* 17:2(1985): 53-63.

Kinsey, J. "Evaluation of a Condom Distribution Program." Paper presented at The American Public Health Association meeting, November 1982.

Kirby, D. *School-based Health Clinics: An Emerging Approach to Improving Adolescent Health and Addressing Teenage Pregnancy.* Washington, DC: Center for Population Options, 1985.

Kirby, D. "The Mathtech Research on Adolescent Sexuality Education Programs." *SIECUS Report* 12:1(September 1983): 11-12, 21-22.

Levine, E., and Thornton, J. "Teen Pregnancy Prevention: Male Involvement in Family Planning Services." Paper presented at Annual Meeting of the American Public Health Association, 1985.

Los Angeles Comprehensive AIDS Risk Reduction Education Service. "Program Report." *Men's Reproductive Health* 1:4(Fall 1987): 8-9.

Lovick, S. *The School-based Clinic Update 1987.* Washington, DC: Support Center for School-based Clinics, 1987.

MacLeaod, J. *Ain't No Makin' It.* Boulder, CO: Westview Press, 1987.

Marsiglio, W. "Adolescent Fathers: A National Portrait and Analysis of Living Arrangements, Marriage, and Educational Outcomes." *Family Planning Perspectives* 19:6(1988): 240-251.

Marsiglio, W., and Mott, F. "The Impact of Sex Education on Sexual Activity, Contraceptive Use and Premarital Pregnancy Among American Teenagers." *Family Planning Perspectives* 18:4 (1986): 151-161.

McAdoo, H. Cited in a speech in Chicago, March 1985.

McCallister, S. Director of Patient Services, Planned Parenthood of Snohomish County. Personal communication with author, 1985.

McMillen, E. Presentation at Conference on School-based Clinics, Kansas City, 1987.

McNally, K. "APHA Task Force Report." *Men's Reproductive Health* 2:1(Winter 1988): 3.

Mescia, N. "Pee Dee District Family Planning Health Education Male Program." Report to South Carolina Health Department for period October 1972-June 1973.

Miller, P.Y., and Simon, W. "The Development of Sexuality in Adolescence." In *Handbook of Adolescent Psychology*. Edited by J. Adelson. New York: Wiley-Interscience, 1980.

Moore, D.; Sluder, H.; and Erickson, D. "A Survey of Unwanted Sexual Experiences." Unpublished paper. 1986.

Mott, F. "Early Fertility Behavior Among American Youth." Paper presented at Annual Meeting of American Public Health Association, Dallas, TX, 1983.

National Center for Health Statistics. *Monthly Vital Statistics Report* 35:4(1986).

National Urban League. *Adolescent Male Responsibility: A Program Development Guide.* New York, 1987.

Oresky, D., and Ewing, E. "Review and Annotated Bibliography of Literature on Male Involvement in Family Planning." National Institute for Community Development, Arlington, VA, January 1978. Mimeo.

Population Information Program. "Barrier Methods." *Population Reports*, series H, no. G (1982).

Ridgely, J.S. "Health Means Jobs." *World Health* (January/February 1985).

Sanders, J., and Rosen, J. "Teenage Fathers: Working with the Neglected Partner in Adolescent Childbearing." *Family Planning Perspectives* 19:3(1987): 107-110.

Scales, P., and Beckstein, D. "From Macho to Mutuality: Helping Young Men Make Effective Decisions about Sex, Contraception and Pregnancy." In *Pregnancy in Adolescence: Needs, Problems and Management.* Edited by I. Stuart and C. Wells. New York: Van Nostrand, 1982.

Schott, S. "PP: Involves Men." *Planned Parenthood Review* (Spring 1981).

Shostak, A.B. "Abortion as Fatherhood Lost: Problems and Reforms." *Family Coordinator* (October 1979).

Smith, P. "Adolescent Sexuality." In *Adolescent Reproductive Health.* Edited by P. Smith and D. Mumford. New York: Gardner Press, 1985.

Smith, P., and Kolenda, K. "Adolescent Male Reproduction." In *Adolescent Reproductive Health.* Edited by P. Smith and D. Mumford. New York: Gardner Press, 1985.

Stuart, I., and Wells, C., eds. *Pregnancy in Adolescence: Need, Problems and Management.* New York: Van Nostrand, 1982.

Sullivan, M. "Teen Fathers in the Inner City: An Exploratory Ethnographic Study." A report to the Ford Foundation, April 1985.

Swanson, J.M. "Shared Contraception." In *Men's Reproductive Health.* Edited by J.M. Swanson and K.A. Forrest. New York: Springer Publishing Company, 1984.

Swanson, J.M., and Forrest, K. "Men's Reproductive Services in Family Planning Settings: A Pilot Study." *American Journal Public Health* 77:11(1987): 1462-1463.

Talbot, J.M.; Rohrbach, L.; Coan, C.; and Kar, S. "The Status of Teen Peer Advocate Programs in the U.S." Los Angeles Regional Family Planning Council, January, 1982. Mimeo.

Udry, J.; Billy, J.; Morris, N.; Groff, T.; and Raj, M. "Serum Androgenic Hormones Motivate Sexual Behavior in Adolescent Boys." *Fertility and Sterility* 43(1985): 90-94.

U.S. Bureau of the Census. *Poverty in the U.S. 1985.* Current Population Reports, Series P-60, No. 158, Washington, DC:USGPO, October 1987.

U.S. Bureau of the Census. *Statistical Abstract of the United States: 1987*, Washington, DC, 1986a.

U.S. Bureau of the Census. *School Enrollment—Social and Economic Characteristics of Students: October 1985 (Advance Report).* Current Population Reports, Series P-20, 409. Washington, DC:USGPO, September 1986b.

U.S. Congress. Senate. Children's Public Policy Forum on Comprehensive School-based Clinics. Held June 5, 1985. Testimony from witnesses. (Also published in the Congressional Record).

Vaz, R.; Smolen, P.; and Miller, C. "Adolescent Pregnancy: Involvement of the Male Partner." *Journal of Adolescent Health Care* 4:4(1983).

Watson, A., and Haffner, D.W. *Implementing a Young Men's Sexuality Education Program: A How to Guide.* Washington, DC: Planned Parenthood of Metropolitan Washington, 1984.

Zabin, L.S.; Hirsch, M.B.; Smith, E.A.; and Hardy, J.B. "Sexual Attitudes and Behavior: Are They Consistent." *Family Planning Perspectives* 16:4(1984): 181-185.

Zabin, L.S.; Hirsch, M.B.; Smith, E.A.; Streett, R.; and Hardy, J.B. "Evaluation of a Pregnancy Prevention Program for Urban Teenagers." *Family Planning Perspectives* 18:3(1986): 119-129.

Zelnik, M., and Shah, F. "First Intercourse among Young Americans." *Family Planning Perspectives* 15:2(1983): 64-70.

Zelnik, M., and Kim, Y.J. "Sex Education and its Association with Teenage Sexual Activity, Pregnancy and Contraceptive Use." *Family Planning Perspectives* 14:3(1982): 117-123.

Zelnik, M., and Kantner, J.F. "Sexual Activity, Contraceptive Use and Pregnancy Among Metropolitan-area Teenagers: 1971- 1979." *Family Planning Perspectives* 12:5(1980): 230-237.

1·18·89

About the Author

Joy G. Dryfoos is a researcher, writer and lecturer from Hastings-on-Hudson, New York. She has received support from the Carnegie Corporation since 1984 to study adolescent males and to summarize the state-of-the-art in prevention programs, with a focus on all adolescents at risk. Dryfoos was formerly associated with The Alan Guttmacher Institute. She has taught at the Columbia University School of Public Health and serves on many advisory panels concerned with youth including the National Academy of Sciences, New York State Education Department, Girls Clubs of America, and the American Public Health Association.

Putting the Boys in the Picture is the first publication ever to focus entirely on intervention strategies for boys to prevent teen pregnancies. Based on an extensive survey of existing male involvement programs and services in the United States, this report includes model programs for making contraception and AIDS prevention information available to teenage boys. Sex education, decision making and life planning, teen peer advocate programs, teen theatre, condom distribution and comprehensive health and social services are among the subjects covered in this comprehensive review.

For use in clinics, schools, youth-serving agencies and male outreach programs, **Putting the Boys in the Picture** includes:

- ✓ A review of current literature on male involvement
- ✓ Information from boys, extracted from self-reported life experiences
- ✓ Statistical data on social/economic status of boys
- ✓ Research on determinants of teen pregnancy, namely
  - *Initiation of sexual activity*
  - *Use of contraception*
  - *Attitudes toward pregnancy*
- ✓ Experiences of teen fatherhood
- ✓ Programs
- ✓ Organizational strategies
- ✓ Priorities for action
- ✓ References

Network Publications, a division of ETR Associates
Santa Cruz, CA

ISBN: 0-941816-55-9